Linux Advanced for SysAdmin

Become a proficient system administrator to manage networks, database, system health, automation and kubernetes

Ryan Juan

Published by: GitforGits

Publisher: Sonal Dhandre

www.gitforgits.com

support@gitforgits.com

Printed in India

First Printing: May 2024

ISBN: 9788119177851

Cover Design by: Kitten Publishing

Prologue

After completing the first book, *Linux Basics for SysAdmin*, I was eager to dive into the next level of Linux system administration. The foundational knowledge provided in that book was essential for setting the stage for more advanced topics. It covered crucial skills such as navigating the Linux filesystem, managing user accounts, handling basic security measures, and performing routine system tasks. With that strong base, readers are now ready to explore the more sophisticated aspects of system administration.

Linux Advanced for SysAdmin is designed to elevate your expertise, focusing on the intricate tasks critical for managing enterprise-level Linux environments. This book is structured to provide comprehensive insights and practical experiences across seven key areas, transforming you into a proficient and capable system administrator.

We begin with **Up and Running with System Administration Essentials**, a quick refresher to ensure you're prepared for advanced topics. This chapter revisits crucial administrative tasks like browsing files and directories, managing packages, using systemd, and configuring user profiles and permissions. It sets the stage for more complex learning and ensures you are up to speed with the basics before diving into advanced topics.

In **Managing Networks**, you will learn to configure and manage network interfaces, IP addresses, and routing. You'll delve into essential network services like DHCP and DNS, and use tools like Wireshark for network diagnostics. This chapter also covers network security, ensuring you can maintain robust and secure network environments.

Security and Monitoring delves into advanced security practices. You'll configure firewalls with **iptables** and **firewalld**, implement AppArmor, and perform security audits with Lynis. You'll also set up intrusion detection systems like Snort and monitor system logs for security issues, fortifying your systems against threats and ensuring compliance with security standards.

Database Management will equip you with skills to handle databases in Linux environments, focusing on PostgreSQL. You'll master installation, configuration, database design, migrations, backup and restore procedures, and performance monitoring with Nagios. This chapter ensures you can manage and secure databases efficiently and effectively.

System Health Monitoring covers techniques for monitoring CPU, memory, disk usage, and network performance. You'll use tools like **top**, **htop**, Nagios, and Zabbix to maintain system health and uptime. This chapter emphasizes the importance of proactive monitoring and the ability to respond quickly to system performance issues.

In **Automation and Scripting**, you'll enhance your scripting skills to automate routine tasks, manage resources, and perform system audits. You'll use shell scripting, **cron**, **anacron**, **awk**, and **sed** to achieve efficient automation. This chapter highlights the power of automation in reducing manual workloads and increasing system reliability.

Finally, **Advanced System Administration** explores managing large-scale deployments, Kubernetes, cluster management, load balancing, and kernel customization. These advanced topics will prepare you to handle the most complex and demanding environments with confidence and expertise. You'll learn to deploy and manage applications at scale, ensure high availability, and optimize system performance through kernel customization.

This journey will transform you into a proficient and capable system administrator, ready to tackle the challenges of modern IT infrastructure. By mastering these advanced topics, you will be well-equipped to manage and optimize large-scale Linux environments, ensuring their security, performance, and reliability.

Content

Preface

"Linux Advanced for SysAdmin" is a comprehensive guide tailored for those who seek to master the complex and advanced aspects of Linux system administration. Building upon fundamental Linux skills, this book is designed to elevate your expertise to handle intricate tasks crucial for senior system administrators.

In **Chapter 1: Up and Running with System Administration Essentials**, you will revisit key administrative tasks, providing a solid foundation for the advanced topics to come. This includes managing files, directories, packages, system services, and user permissions to ensure you're up to speed. **Chapter 2: Managing Networks** dives into the critical aspects of network management. You will learn to configure network interfaces, manage IP addresses and routing, set up and secure network services like DHCP and DNS, and monitor network performance using tools such as Wireshark. This chapter ensures you can maintain robust network environments essential for any enterprise.

Chapter 3: Security and Monitoring focuses on implementing robust security measures. You will explore **iptables** and **firewalld**, configure firewalls, implement AppArmor, and perform security audits with Lynis. The chapter also covers monitoring system logs for security breaches and using intrusion detection systems like Snort. In **Chapter 4: Database Management**, you will learn to work with databases in Linux, including installing and configuring PostgreSQL, designing databases, performing migrations, and securing database systems. This chapter equips you with the skills to manage database operations efficiently.

Chapter 5: System Health Monitoring teaches you to monitor CPU and memory usage, track network performance, and analyze system logs using tools like Nagios and Zabbix. You will also learn to set up alerts and notifications to maintain optimal system performance. **Chapter 6: Automation and Scripting** focuses on automating routine tasks using shell scripting, **cron**, **anacron**, **awk**, and **sed**. You will learn to write scripts for system audits, resource management, and backup and recovery.

Finally, **Chapter 7: Advanced System Administration** covers large-scale deployments, Kubernetes, cluster management, load balancing, and kernel customization. These topics are crucial for managing extensive and high-demand Linux environments.

You will finish this book with a solid foundation in advanced Linux administration and the self-assurance to tackle even the most daunting tasks. In order to become a competent system administrator, this book is essential reading.

In this book you will learn how to:

- Master large-scale deployments to ensure efficient and consistent application management across multiple servers.

- Use Kubernetes to your advantage for reliable application scaling and smooth container orchestration.
- Optimize resource utilization, set up scalability, and ensure high availability by managing clusters.
- Improve your service's performance and dependability with sophisticated load balancing strategies.
- Personalize Linux's kernel in terms of speed, security, and hardware compatibility.
- Automate complex tasks with shell scripting, cron, and anacron.
- Get the most out of AppArmor, firewalld, and iptables to boost up security.
- Take advantage of Nagios, Zabbix, and Wireshark to keep your systems and networks running smoothly.
- Get PostgreSQL up and running, migrate databases, and automate routine tasks; all while keeping databases secure.
- Learn to resolve complex issues and maintain system health and uptime with significant troubleshooting skills.

GitforGits

Prerequisites

If you're interested in learning more about Linux and want to advance your skills beyond the basics, this book will teach you everything you need to become a SysAdmin, or powerful Linux administrator, and control the Linux systems in your organization with ease.

Codes Usage

Are you in need of some helpful code examples to assist you in your programming and documentation? Look no further! Our book offers a wealth of supplemental material, including code examples and exercises.

Not only is this book here to aid you in getting your job done, but you have our permission to use the example code in your programs and documentation. However, please note that if you are reproducing a significant portion of the code, we do require you to contact us for permission.

But don't worry, using several chunks of code from this book in your program or answering a question by citing our book and quoting example code does not require permission. But if you do choose to give credit, an attribution typically includes the title, author, publisher, and ISBN. For example, "Linux Advanced for SysAdmin by Ryan Juan".

If you are unsure whether your intended use of the code examples falls under fair use or the permissions outlined above, please do not hesitate to reach out to us at support@gitforgits.com.

We are happy to assist and clarify any concerns.

Acknowledgement

I owe a tremendous debt of gratitude to GitforGits, for their unflagging enthusiasm and wise counsel throughout the entire process of writing this book. Their knowledge and careful editing helped make sure the piece was useful for people of all reading levels and comprehension skills. In addition, I'd like to thank everyone involved in the publishing process for their efforts in making this book a reality. Their efforts, from copyediting to advertising, made the project what it is today.

Finally, I'd like to express my gratitude to everyone who has shown me unconditional love and encouragement throughout my life. Their support was crucial to the completion of this book. I appreciate your help with this endeavour and your continued interest in my career.

Chapter 1: Up and Running with System Administration Essentials

Overview

This chapter serves as a quick refresher to get you up to speed with the fundamental aspects of Linux system administration before diving into the advanced topics covered in this book. It is designed to provide a brief overview and practical demonstration of essential tasks such as browsing files and directories, using commands, managing packages, utilizing systemd, scheduling tasks with crontab, automating tasks with at and batch, and managing user profiles and permissions including ACL and PAM.

We understand that the pace of this chapter might be fast for some readers, especially those who are not yet familiar with these basic tasks. If you find it challenging to grasp these essentials and feel the need to strengthen your understanding of the foundational concepts covered in this chapter, we highly recommend reading our companion book, "Linux Basics for SysAdmin," published on 23 May 2024. This book offers a comprehensive introduction to Linux system administration, covering fundamental topics in greater detail and at a more gradual pace. It will provide you with the essential knowledge and confidence needed to successfully navigate the advanced aspects of Linux administration presented in the subsequent chapters of this book.

"Linux Basics for SysAdmin" is not only beneficial for beginners but also serves as a valuable resource for experienced Linux administrators. Even seasoned professionals can find the book useful for revisiting core concepts, refining their command-line skills, and exploring foundational practices that ensure a robust understanding of Linux systems. The book covers a wide range of topics including navigating the Linux filesystem, using basic commands, managing files and directories, understanding the shell, package management, system startup and shutdown, process management, and accessing Linux utilities.

Introduction to AlphaProject

Brief Overview

AlphaProject is an ambitious initiative designed to streamline and automate key aspects of system administration. The project's primary goal is to create a robust, scalable, and secure infrastructure that supports various applications and services essential to an organization. As a system administrator, your role in AlphaProject is crucial, involving tasks such as managing servers, ensuring network reliability, implementing security measures, and maintaining system performance.

AlphaProject is built on a Linux-based environment, leveraging the flexibility and power of open-source technologies. The project encompasses a wide range of components, including web servers, databases, file systems, and network configurations. Your responsibilities will include configuring these components, monitoring their performance, and troubleshooting issues that arise.

Skillset of SysAdmin for AlphaProject

To effectively manage AlphaProject, a system administrator needs a diverse set of skills. These skills can be broadly categorized into the following areas:

1. Linux Proficiency: A deep understanding of the Linux operating system, including command-line operations, file system navigation, and basic scripting, is essential.
2. Network Management: Knowledge of networking concepts, including IP addressing, routing, and managing network services (e.g., DHCP, DNS), is crucial for maintaining connectivity and ensuring efficient data flow.
3. Security Implementation: Implementing security measures such as firewalls, intrusion detection systems, and access controls is vital to protect the infrastructure from threats.
4. System Monitoring: The ability to monitor system performance, analyze logs, and set up alerts is important for maintaining the health of the infrastructure.
5. Automation and Scripting: Proficiency in writing scripts to automate routine tasks, manage configurations, and deploy updates enhances efficiency and reduces manual intervention.
6. Database Management: Managing databases, including installation, configuration, and performance tuning, ensures that applications can access and store data reliably.
7. Virtualization and Containerization: Experience with virtualization technologies (e.g., VirtualBox, VMware) and containerization (e.g., Docker) is beneficial for creating isolated environments for testing and deployment.
8. Backup and Recovery: Setting up and managing backup solutions to ensure data integrity and recoverability in case of failures.
9. Troubleshooting: Strong problem-solving skills to diagnose and resolve issues quickly, minimizing downtime and ensuring continuous service availability.

Exploring AlphaProject Components

Browsing Files and Directories

Navigating the file system is fundamental for any system administrator. You will often need to locate configuration files, log files, and scripts. Using commands like **ls**, **cd**, **pwd**, **find**, and **tree** can help you effectively browse the file system.

- List Directory Contents:

```
$ ls /projects/AlphaProject
```

- Change Directory:

```
$ cd /projects/AlphaProject
```

- Print Working Directory:

```
$ pwd
```

- Find Files:

```
$ find /projects/AlphaProject -name '*.conf'
```

- Display Directory Tree:

```
$ tree /projects/AlphaProject
```

Using Essential Linux Commands

Proficiency with essential Linux commands is critical. Commands like **cp**, **mv**, **rm**, **chmod**, **chown**, **df**, **du**, **ps**, **top**, **grep**, **awk**, and **sed** are frequently used for file operations, permissions management, disk usage analysis, process management, and text processing.

- Copy Files:

```
$ cp /source/file /destination/
```

- Move Files:

```
$ mv /source/file /destination/
```

- Remove Files:

```
$ rm /projects/AlphaProject/tempfile
```

- Change Permissions:

```
$ chmod 755 /projects/AlphaProject/script.sh
```

- Change Ownership:

```
$ chown user:group /projects/AlphaProject/directory
```

- Disk Usage:

```
$ df -h

$ du -sh /projects/AlphaProject
```

- Process Management:

```
$ ps aux

$ top
```

- Text Processing:

```
$ grep 'error' /var/log/syslog

$ awk '{print $1}' /projects/AlphaProject/data.txt

$ sed 's/oldtext/newtext/g'
/projects/AlphaProject/file.txt
```

Managing Packages with 'apt'

Package management is essential for installing, updating, and removing software. In Debian-based systems, **`apt`** is used, while Red Hat-based systems use **`yum`**.

- Update Package Lists:

```
$ sudo apt update

$ sudo yum check-update
```

- Install Packages:

```
$ sudo apt install apache2
```

```
$ sudo yum install httpd
```

- Upgrade Packages:

```
$ sudo apt upgrade

$ sudo yum update
```

- Remove Packages:

```
$ sudo apt remove apache2

$ sudo yum remove httpd
```

Using 'systemd' for Service Management

Systemd is a system and service manager for Linux, responsible for initializing the system, managing system services, and handling system resources.

- Start a Service:

```
$ sudo systemctl start apache2
```

- Stop a Service:

```
$ sudo systemctl stop apache2
```

- Enable a Service:

```
$ sudo systemctl enable apache2
```

- Disable a Service:

```
$ sudo systemctl disable apache2
```

- Check Service Status:

```
$ sudo systemctl status apache2
```

Scheduling Tasks with 'crontab'

Cron jobs are used to schedule repetitive tasks. The **crontab** command allows you to manage cron jobs.

- Edit Crontab:

```
$ crontab -e
```

Add a cron job to run a script every day at midnight:

```
0 0 * * * /projects/AlphaProject/script.sh
```

- List Crontab:

```
$ crontab -l
```

Automating Tasks with 'at' and 'batch'

The **at** and **batch** commands are used for one-time task scheduling.

- Schedule a Task with **at**:

```
$ echo "/projects/AlphaProject/script.sh" | at 02:00
```

- View Scheduled **at** Jobs:

```
$ atq
```

- Remove Scheduled **at** Job:

```
$ atrm job_number
```

- Schedule a Batch Job:

```
$ echo "/projects/AlphaProject/script.sh" | batch
```

Managing User Profiles and Permissions

Managing user profiles and permissions ensures secure access control.

- Create a User:

```
$ sudo useradd -m -s /bin/bash user1

$ sudo passwd user1
```

- Add User to Group:

```
$ sudo usermod -aG sudo user1
```

- Modify User Profile:

```
$ sudo usermod -d /home/newdir user1
```

- Set File Permissions:

```
$ chmod 755 /projects/AlphaProject/file.txt
```

- Change File Ownership:

```
$ chown user1:developers /projects/AlphaProject/file.txt
```

Implementing ACLs (Access Control Lists)

ACLs provide more granular control over file permissions.

- Set ACL for a User:

```
$ sudo setfacl -m u:user1:rwx
/projects/AlphaProject/file.txt
```

- View ACLs:

```
$ getfacl /projects/AlphaProject/file.txt
```

Working with Pluggable Authentication Modules (PAM)

PAM allows you to manage authentication and security policies.

Configure PAM for SSH

- Edit **/etc/pam.d/sshd**:

```
auth required pam_google_authenticator.so
```

Set Password Quality

- Edit **/etc/pam.d/common-password**:

```
password requisite pam_pwquality.so retry=3 minlen=12
dcredit=-1 ucredit=-1 ocredit=-1 lcredit=-1
```

By getting yourself well acquainted and practiced around these essentials, you will be sufficiently comfortable to dive into the advanced topics aimed to teach you in this book.

Summary

In the upcoming chapters of this book, you will explore advanced aspects of Linux administration, including network management, security and monitoring, database management, system health monitoring, automation and scripting, and advanced system administration. You'll learn to configure IP addresses, manage network services, set up firewalls, implement SELinux, perform security audits, manage MySQL and PostgreSQL databases, monitor system performance, automate tasks with scripts, and handle large-scale deployments with Kubernetes.

The rapid learning on the prerequisite provided by this chapter fulfills a crucial refresher on essential system administration tasks, ensuring you have a solid foundation. By revisiting these basics, you will be well-prepared to tackle the advanced topics with confidence and ease, making the learning process smoother and more efficient.

CHAPTER 2: MANAGING NETWORKS

Introduction

Part of being a good system administrator is being able to manage networks, and in this chapter, "Managing Networks," you will learn how it is done. Understanding network interfaces, the building blocks of Linux network connectivity, will be your first step. You can ensure that your systems can communicate both internally and outside by learning to configure IP addresses and routing. This will enable you to set up and manage network communication successfully.

The next step is to learn how to administer network services like NFS, DNS, and DHCP. Domain name resolution, file sharing across networks, and dynamic IP address allocation are three services that are absolutely necessary. You will learn to detect network faults using tools like traceroute and ping, which will help you maintain a healthy network environment.

In this chapter, you will learn how to set up network file systems, which will make sharing files across many platforms simple and straightforward. By keeping an eye on network traffic with Wireshark, you may examine data from your network and spot unusual activity. We will put a lot of emphasis on troubleshooting network difficulties so that you may learn to recognize and fix typical network problems.

Lastly, you will gain knowledge of wireless network management and how to build high availability to keep your network services operational despite hardware failures or other interruptions. In order to ensure that AlphaProject and other enterprise environments run well, it is essential to have a solid network infrastructure. This chapter will teach you what you need to know about network management.

Understanding Network Interfaces

The ability to communicate between devices that are part of a network is made possible via network interfaces, which are essential components of any computing environment. The kind of connection they enable determines whether they are physical or virtual. Being able to manage and troubleshoot network connectivity efficiently requires knowledge of the many kinds of network interfaces and what makes them unique.

Types of Network Interfaces

Ethernet Interfaces (ethX)

- These are the most common network interfaces in business environments, typically representing wired connections. Examples include **eth0**, **eth1**, etc.
- They are used for high-speed data transfer over wired connections and are usually connected via network cables to switches, routers, or directly to other devices.

Wireless Interfaces (wlanX)

- Representing wireless connections, these interfaces are denoted as **wlan0, wlan1**, etc.
- They connect to wireless networks and are essential for laptops, mobile devices, and other wireless-capable devices.

Loopback Interface (lo)

- A special virtual network interface used for internal communication within the host. The IP address **127.0.0.1** is typically associated with the loopback interface.
- It is used for testing and development purposes, allowing network services to communicate within the same device.

Virtual Interfaces (vnetX, virbrX)

- Used in virtualized environments, these interfaces connect virtual machines (VMs) to the network. Examples include **vnet0**, **virbr0**, etc.
- They are critical for cloud computing and virtualized server environments, providing network connectivity to VMs.

Bridge Interfaces (brX)

- These interfaces connect multiple network segments and operate at the data link layer. They are often used in virtualization and containerized environments.
- Bridges like **br0** combine several interfaces into a single logical network segment.

Bonded Interfaces (bondX)

- Bonding (or teaming) combines multiple network interfaces into a single logical interface to increase bandwidth and provide redundancy. Examples include **bond0, bond1**, etc.
- Bonding is used for high availability and load balancing in enterprise networks.

Tunnel Interfaces (tunX, tapX)

- These interfaces are used for creating VPN tunnels. Examples include **tun0**, **tap0**, etc.
- They enable encrypted communication across untrusted networks.

Container Network Interfaces (cniX)

- Used in containerized environments like Docker and Kubernetes. Examples include **cni0**, **cni1**, etc.
- They provide network connectivity to containers, ensuring that each container can communicate with other containers and external networks.

Key Elements SysAdmin Must Know

To manage AlphaProject or any networked environment effectively, a system administrator should be well-versed with the following information about network interfaces:

Interface Names and Types

Knowing the names and types of all network interfaces in use (e.g., **eth0**, **wlan0**, **lo**) is fundamental. This information is crucial for configuring and troubleshooting network connections.

MAC Addresses

The MAC (Media Access Control) address is a unique identifier for each network interface. It is essential for network configuration and security.
Below is an example:

```
$ ip link show eth0
```

IP Addresses

IP addresses assigned to each network interface, including IPv4 and IPv6 addresses. Understanding which IP addresses are static and which are dynamic (DHCP) is crucial.
Below is an example:

```
$ ip addr show eth0
```

Subnet Masks and CIDR Notation

Subnet masks define the network and host portions of an IP address. CIDR (Classless Inter-Domain Routing) notation is used for IP addressing and routing.
Below is an example:

```
$ ip addr show eth0 | grep inet
```

Default Gateway

The default gateway is the router that connects the local network to other networks, including the internet. Knowing the default gateway is essential for network routing.
Below is an example:

```
$ ip route show
```

DNS Servers

DNS (Domain Name System) servers resolve domain names to IP addresses. Configuration of DNS servers is crucial for network connectivity.
Below is an example:

```
$ cat /etc/resolv.conf
```

MTU (Maximum Transmission Unit)

MTU defines the maximum packet size that can be transmitted over a network interface. Incorrect MTU settings can cause network issues.
Below is an example:

```
$ ip link show eth0 | grep mtu
```

Status and Statistics

The operational status (up or down) and statistics such as packet loss, errors, and collisions provide insights into network performance and issues.
Below is an example:

```
$ ip -s link show eth0
```

VLAN Configuration

VLANs (Virtual Local Area Networks) allow network segmentation. Understanding VLAN configuration on network interfaces is important for network organization and security.
Below is an example:

```
$ ip link add link eth0 name eth0.100 type vlan id 100
```

Bonding and Bridging

Configuration details of bonded and bridged interfaces, including their modes and member interfaces, are crucial for network redundancy and load balancing.
Below is an example:

```
$ cat /proc/net/bonding/bond0
```

Firewall Rules

Understanding how firewall rules are applied to network interfaces to control traffic flow and enhance security.
Below is an example:

```
$ sudo iptables -L -v -n
```

Sample Program: Gathering Information of All Network Interfaces

- List All Network Interfaces

```
$ ip link show
```

- Check IP Address Configuration

```
$ ip addr show
```

- Display Routing Table

```
$ ip route show
```

- View DNS Configuration

```
$ cat /etc/resolv.conf
```

- Check Interface Statistics

```
$ ip -s link show eth0
```

- Show VLAN Configuration

```
$ ip -d link show eth0
```

- Display Bonding Configuration

```
$ cat /proc/net/bonding/bond0
```

- View Firewall Rules

```
$ sudo iptables -L -v -n
```

When you have a good grasp of these features of network interfaces, you will be better equipped to set up, examine, and fix network connections. In your capacity as a system administrator for AlphaProject, possessing this knowledge guarantees your ability to uphold a resilient and dependable network infrastructure, which facilitates uninterrupted data transmission and communication throughout the organization.

Configuring IP Addresses and Routing

Prior to a network that can be used for internal or external communication, IP addresses and routing must be configured. Here, we will show you how to navigate when it comes to configuring IP addresses and routing, so you can get your network talking to each other and the outside world in no time.

Configuring IP Addresses

IP addresses are unique identifiers assigned to each device on a network, allowing them to communicate. Following is the example of how you can configure IP addresses on your Linux system.

Assigning Static IP Address

To assign a static IP address, you can use the **ip** command. The below code snippet configures a static IP address on the **eth0** interface.

```
$ sudo ip addr add 192.168.1.100/24 dev eth0
```

This command assigns the IP address **192.168.1.100** with a subnet mask of **255.255.255.0** to the **eth0** interface.

Removing IP Address

If you need to remove an IP address, use the following command:

```
$ sudo ip addr del 192.168.1.100/24 dev eth0
```

Configuring IP Address via netplan

For a persistent configuration, use **netplan**. Edit the YAML configuration file typically located in **/etc/netplan/**.

```
$ sudo nano /etc/netplan/01-netcfg.yaml
```

- Add the following configuration:

```
network:
 version: 2
 ethernets:
 eth0:
 dhcp4: no
 addresses:
 - 192.168.1.100/24
 gateway4: 192.168.1.1
 nameservers:
 addresses:
 - 8.8.8.8
 - 8.8.4.4
```

- Apply the configuration:

```
$ sudo netplan apply
```

Configuring Routing

Routing directs packets between different networks. Proper routing configuration ensures that data is sent to the correct destination efficiently. Following is the example of how to configure routing on your Linux system.

Viewing the Current Routing Table

Use the **ip route** command to view the current routing table:

```
$ ip route show
```

Following is the sample output:

```
default via 192.168.1.1 dev eth0 proto static

192.168.1.0/24 dev eth0 proto kernel scope link src
192.168.1.100
```

Adding a Default Route

A default route is used to send packets to destinations not specified in the routing table. The following command sets a default route via the gateway **192.168.1.1**:

```
$ sudo ip route add default via 192.168.1.1
```

Adding a Static Route

Static routes are used for directing packets to specific networks. The below code snippet adds a route to the network **10.0.0.0/24** via the gateway **192.168.1.254**:

```
$ sudo ip route add 10.0.0.0/24 via 192.168.1.254
```

Deleting a Route

To delete a route, use the following command:

```
$ sudo ip route del 10.0.0.0/24 via 192.168.1.254
```

Configuring Persistent Routes

To make routes persistent across reboots, add them to the network configuration files. For example, on Ubuntu, edit the **/etc/netplan/01-netcfg.yaml** file:

```
network:
```

```
version: 2
ethernets:
eth0:
dhcp4: no
addresses:
- 192.168.1.100/24
gateway4: 192.168.1.1
nameservers:
addresses:
- 8.8.8.8
- 8.8.4.4
routes:
- to: 10.0.0.0/24
via: 192.168.1.254
```

Apply the configuration:

```
$ sudo netplan apply
```

Routing Best Practices

Renowned routing practices in IT environments include dynamic routing protocols and redundant paths to ensure network resilience and efficiency.

Dynamic Routing Protocols

Dynamic routing protocols like OSPF (Open Shortest Path First) and BGP (Border Gateway Protocol) automatically adjust routes based on network changes. While these are typically configured on routers, understanding them is essential for network administrators.

Routing with Quagga

Quagga is a software suite that provides implementations of OSPF, BGP, and other routing protocols.

- Install Quagga:

```
$ sudo apt install quagga
```

- Configure Quagga:

Edit the configuration files in **/etc/quagga/**, such as **zebra.conf** and **ospfd.conf**. Following is the example for `zebra.conf`:

```
hostname Router

password zebra

enable password zebra

log file /var/log/quagga/zebra.log
```

Following is the example for `ospfd.conf`:

```
hostname ospfd

password zebra

log file /var/log/quagga/ospfd.log


router ospf

 network 192.168.1.0/24 area 0.0.0.0

 network 10.0.0.0/24 area 0.0.0.0
```

- Enable and start Quagga services:

```
$ sudo systemctl enable zebra

$ sudo systemctl start zebra

$ sudo systemctl enable ospfd

$ sudo systemctl start ospfd
```

Redundant Paths and High Availability

Implementing redundant paths using techniques like VRRP (Virtual Router Redundancy Protocol) ensures high availability.

- Install Keepalived:

```
$ sudo apt install keepalived
```

- Configure Keepalived:

Edit the /etc/keepalived/keepalived.conf file. Following is the sample configuration:

```
vrrp_instance VI_1 {

 state MASTER

 interface eth0

 virtual_router_id 51

 priority 100

 advert_int 1

 authentication {

 auth_type PASS

 auth_pass password

 }

 virtual_ipaddress {
```

```
 192.168.1.200
 }
}
```

- Start and enable Keepalived:

```
$ sudo systemctl start keepalived
$ sudo systemctl enable keepalived
```

Sample Program: Configuring Routing for Internal/External Communication

Configuring Internal Communication

Assign IP addresses and routes within the AlphaProject network to ensure internal communication. Following is the example on configuring the **eth0** interface:

```
$ sudo ip addr add 10.1.1.1/24 dev eth0
$ sudo ip route add 10.1.2.0/24 via 10.1.1.254
```

Setting up External Communication

Configure external communication by setting up a default gateway and DNS servers. Following is the example to add a default route and DNS configuration:

```
$ sudo ip route add default via 192.168.1.1
$ echo "nameserver 8.8.8.8" | sudo tee /etc/resolv.conf
$ echo "nameserver 8.8.4.4" | sudo tee -a
/etc/resolv.conf
```

Implementing Persistent Configuration

- Ensure configurations are persistent across reboots using **netplan** or **nmcli**. For example:

```
network:
 version: 2
 ethernets:
 eth0:
 dhcp4: no
 addresses:
 - 10.1.1.1/24
 gateway4: 192.168.1.1
 nameservers:
 addresses:
 - 8.8.8.8
 - 8.8.4.4
 routes:
 - to: 10.1.2.0/24
 via: 10.1.1.254
```

- Apply the configuration:

```
$ sudo netplan apply
```

The proper configuration of IP addresses and routing creates a strong network architecture that allows AlphaProject to communicate internally and externally efficiently. Your network's capacity to respond to changes and maintain high availability is dependent on your understanding and implementation of routing strategies.

Managing Network Services

Managing network services like DHCP, DNS, and NFS is crucial for any IT environment, including AlphaProject, to ensure that network activities run smoothly and that resources are shared efficiently. Using these services, tasks like file sharing, domain name resolution, and dynamic IP address allocation become much easier to accomplish.

Dynamic Host Configuration Protocol (DHCP)

DHCP is a network management protocol used to automate the process of configuring devices on IP networks, allowing them to use dynamically assigned IP addresses and network configurations.

Installing DHCP Server

```
$ sudo apt update

$ sudo apt install isc-dhcp-server
```

Configuring DHCP Server

- Edit the DHCP configuration file, typically located at **`/etc/dhcp/dhcpd.conf`**.

```
$ sudo nano /etc/dhcp/dhcpd.conf
```

- Add the following configuration to define the DHCP range and options:

```
subnet 192.168.1.0 netmask 255.255.255.0 {
 range 192.168.1.100 192.168.1.200;
 option routers 192.168.1.1;
 option subnet-mask 255.255.255.0;
 option domain-name-servers 8.8.8.8, 8.8.4.4;
 option domain-name "gitforgits.com";
}
```

Starting DHCP Service

- Start and enable the DHCP service:

```
$ sudo systemctl start isc-dhcp-server

$ sudo systemctl enable isc-dhcp-server
```

- Verify the DHCP service status:

```
$ sudo systemctl status isc-dhcp-server
```

Sample Program: Setting up DHCP for AlphaProject

Edit the configuration file:

```
$ sudo apt install isc-dhcp-server

$ sudo nano /etc/dhcp/dhcpd.conf
```

Add the configuration:

```
subnet 10.0.0.0 netmask 255.255.255.0 {

 range 10.0.0.100 10.0.0.200;

 option routers 10.0.0.1;

 option subnet-mask 255.255.255.0;

 option domain-name-servers 10.0.0.1;

 option domain-name "alphaproject.local";

}
```

Start the DHCP service:

```
$ sudo systemctl start isc-dhcp-server
```

```
$ sudo systemctl enable isc-dhcp-server
```

Verify the DHCP service status:

```
$ sudo systemctl status isc-dhcp-server
```

Domain Name System (DNS)

DNS translates domain names to IP addresses, enabling users to access websites using human-readable addresses instead of numeric IP addresses.

Installing DNS Server (Bind9)

```
$ sudo apt update

$ sudo apt install bind9
```

Configuring DNS Server

Edit the named configuration file, typically located at **/etc/bind/named.conf.options**.

```
$ sudo nano /etc/bind/named.conf.options
```

Add the following configuration to specify DNS options:

```
options {

 directory "/var/cache/bind";

 forwarders {

 8.8.8.8;

 8.8.4.4;

 };

 dnssec-validation auto;

 listen-on-v6 { any; };
```

```
};
```

Define a zone file in /etc/bind/named.conf.local:

```
zone "gitforgits.com" {
 type master;
 file "/etc/bind/zones/db.gitforgits.com";
};
```

Create the zone file /etc/bind/zones/db.gitforgits.com:

```
$ sudo mkdir /etc/bind/zones
$ sudo nano /etc/bind/zones/db.gitforgits.com
```

Add the following content to the zone file:

```
$TTL 86400
@ IN SOA ns1.gitforgits.com. admin.gitforgits.com. (
 2024052301 ; Serial
 3600 ; Refresh
 1800 ; Retry
 1209600 ; Expire
 86400 ) ; Minimum TTL

@ IN NS ns1.gitforgits.com.
@ IN A 192.168.1.100
```

```
ns1 IN A 192.168.1.100
```

Starting DNS Service

Start and enable the DNS service:

```
$ sudo systemctl start bind9

$ sudo systemctl enable bind9
```

Verify the DNS service status:

```
$ sudo systemctl status bind9
```

Testing DNS Configuration

Use the **dig** or **nslookup** command to test the DNS configuration:

```
$ dig gitforgits.com

$ nslookup gitforgits.com
```

Sample Program: Setting up DNS for AlphaProject

Edit the named options file:

```
$ sudo apt install bind9

$ sudo nano /etc/bind/named.conf.options
```

Add the configuration:

```
options {

 directory "/var/cache/bind";

 forwarders {

 8.8.8.8;
```

```
 8.8.4.4;
 };
 dnssec-validation auto;
 listen-on-v6 { any; };
};
```

Define the zone file:

```
$ sudo nano /etc/bind/named.conf.local
```

Add the zone definition:

```
zone "alphaproject.local" {
 type master;
 file "/etc/bind/zones/db.alphaproject.local";
};
```

Create the zone file:

```
$ sudo mkdir /etc/bind/zones
$ sudo nano /etc/bind/zones/db.alphaproject.local
```

Add the following content:

```
$TTL 86400
@ IN SOA ns1.alphaproject.local.
admin.alphaproject.local. (
 2024052301 ; Serial
```

```
 3600 ; Refresh

 1800 ; Retry

 1209600 ; Expire

 86400 ) ; Minimum TTL


@ IN NS ns1.alphaproject.local.

@ IN A 10.0.0.100

ns1 IN A 10.0.0.100
```

Start the DNS service:

```
$ sudo systemctl start bind9

$ sudo systemctl enable bind9
```

Verify the DNS service status:

```
$ sudo systemctl status bind9
```

Test the DNS configuration:

```
$ dig alphaproject.local

$ nslookup alphaproject.local
```

Network File System (NFS)

NFS allows file sharing across a network, enabling multiple clients to access files stored on a central server.

Installing NFS Server

```
$ sudo apt update

$ sudo apt install nfs-kernel-server
```

Configuring NFS Server

Edit the NFS exports file, typically located at **/etc/exports**.

```
$ sudo nano /etc/exports
```

Add the following configuration to define the shared directory and client permissions:

```
/projects/AlphaProject
192.168.1.0/24(rw,sync,no_subtree_check)
```

Starting NFS Service

Start and enable the NFS service:

```
$ sudo systemctl start nfs-kernel-server

$ sudo systemctl enable nfs-kernel-server
```

Verify the NFS service status:

```
$ sudo systemctl status nfs-kernel-server
```

Configuring NFS Client

To access the NFS share from a client, install the NFS client package:

```
$ sudo apt install nfs-common
```

Create a mount point and mount the NFS share:

```
$ sudo mkdir -p /mnt/AlphaProject
```

```
$ sudo mount 192.168.1.100:/projects/AlphaProject
/mnt/AlphaProject
```

To make the mount persistent across reboots, add the following line to **/etc/fstab**:

```
192.168.1.100:/projects/AlphaProject /mnt/AlphaProject
nfs defaults 0 0
```

Sample Program: Setting up NFS for AlphaProject

Edit the exports file:

```
$ sudo apt install nfs-kernel-server

$ sudo nano /etc/exports
```

Add the following configuration:

```
/projects/AlphaProject
10.0.0.0/24(rw,sync,no_subtree_check)
```

Start the NFS service:

```
$ sudo systemctl start nfs-kernel-server

$ sudo systemctl enable nfs-kernel-server
```

Verify the NFS service status:

```
$ sudo systemctl status nfs-kernel-server
```

Install the NFS client package:

```
$ sudo apt install nfs-common
```

Create a mount point and mount the NFS share:

```
$ sudo mkdir -p /mnt/AlphaProject

$ sudo mount 10.0.0.100:/projects/AlphaProject
/mnt/AlphaProject
```

Add the mount to **/etc/fstab** for persistence:

```
10.0.0.100:/projects/AlphaProject /mnt/AlphaProject nfs
defaults 0 0
```

We learned how DHCP, DNS, and NFS automate IP address assignment, resolve domain names, and enable efficient file sharing across the network with the mentioned before sample programs. This ensures that activities run smoothly and without hitches.

Perform Network Diagnosis

System administrators rely on network diagnostics to keep their networks running smoothly and reliably. Connectivity issues, packet loss, latency, and other network-related problems can impact the overall performance of systems and applications. Performing a network diagnostic can assist in discovering the main cause of these problems. When diagnosing a network, it is also important to use a variety of tools and techniques to examine network activity, identify problems, and apply fixes.

Importance of Network Diagnosis

For AlphaProject or any IT environment, maintaining optimal network performance is essential. Network diagnosis allows system administrators to:

- Determine if devices can communicate with each other over the network.
- Understand delays and data loss in network communication.
- Identify the route taken by packets from the source to the destination.
- Detect unauthorized access and potential threats.
- Make adjustments to improve speed and efficiency.

Exploring 'ping'

The **ping** command is a simple yet powerful tool for diagnosing network connectivity issues. It sends ICMP (Internet Control Message Protocol) Echo Request packets to a target host and waits for Echo Reply packets. This helps verify if the target host is reachable and measures the round-trip time.

Basic 'ping' Usage

To check if a host is reachable, use the **ping** command followed by the IP address or hostname of the target.

```
$ ping 192.168.1.1
```

Following is the sample output:

```
PING 192.168.1.1 (192.168.1.1) 56(84) bytes of data.

64 bytes from 192.168.1.1: icmp_seq=1 ttl=64 time=0.234
ms

64 bytes from 192.168.1.1: icmp_seq=2 ttl=64 time=0.218
ms

64 bytes from 192.168.1.1: icmp_seq=3 ttl=64 time=0.211
ms
```

Specifying the Number of Packets

Use the **-c** option to specify the number of packets to send.

```
$ ping -c 4 192.168.1.1
```

Continuous Ping

To continuously ping a host until interrupted, use the **ping** command without the **-c** option.

```
$ ping alphaproject.local
```

Ping with Interval

Use the **-i** option to set the interval between packets.

```
$ ping -i 2 192.168.1.1
```

Ping with Packet Size

Use the **-s** option to specify the size of the packets.

```
$ ping -s 1000 192.168.1.1
```

Interpreting 'ping' Results

- Round-Trip Time (RTT): Indicates the time taken for a packet to travel to the target and back.
- Packet Loss: Shows the percentage of packets lost during transmission.
- TTL (Time to Live): Indicates the number of hops a packet can make before being discarded.

Sample Program: Diagnosing Network Connectivity Issues

To diagnose network connectivity issues within AlphaProject, perform the following steps:

Ping the Gateway

Check if the gateway is reachable.

```
$ ping -c 4 192.168.1.1
```

Ping Internal Hosts

Ping other devices within the AlphaProject network.

```
$ ping -c 4 10.0.0.101

$ ping -c 4 10.0.0.102
```

Ping External Hosts

Check connectivity to external hosts, such as DNS servers or external websites.

```
$ ping -c 4 8.8.8.8

$ ping -c 4 google.com
```

Exploring 'traceroute'

The **traceroute** command traces the path packets take from the source to the destination, displaying each hop along the route. This helps identify where delays or failures occur in the network.

Installing 'traceroute'

```
$ sudo apt update

$ sudo apt install traceroute
```

Basic 'traceroute' Usage

To trace the route to a destination, use the **traceroute** command followed by the IP address or hostname.

```
$ traceroute 192.168.1.1
```

Following is the sample output:

```
traceroute to 192.168.1.1 (192.168.1.1), 30 hops max, 60
byte packets

 1 10.0.0.1 (10.0.0.1) 0.123 ms 0.098 ms 0.089 ms

 2 192.168.1.1 (192.168.1.1) 0.234 ms 0.218 ms 0.211 ms
```

Specifying Maximum Number of Hops

Use the **-m** option to set the maximum number of hops.

```
$ traceroute -m 20 8.8.8.8
```

Using ICMP Instead of UDP

By default, **traceroute** uses UDP packets. Use the **-I** option to use ICMP packets.

```
$ traceroute -I 192.168.1.1
```

Setting the Packet Size

Use the **-s** option to specify the size of the packets.

```
$ traceroute -s 1000 8.8.8.8
```

Interpreting 'traceroute' Results

- Hop Count: The number of hops from the source to the destination.
- Round-Trip Time (RTT): The time taken for packets to travel to each hop and back.
- Star (*): Indicates that the packet timed out or the router is not responding.

Sample Program: Diagnosing Network Path Issues

To diagnose network path issues within AlphaProject, perform the following steps:

Trace the Route to the Gateway

Check the route to the gateway.

```
$ traceroute 192.168.1.1
```

Trace the Route to Internal Hosts

Trace the route to other devices within the AlphaProject network.

```
$ traceroute 10.0.0.101

$ traceroute 10.0.0.102
```

Trace the Route to External Hosts

Check the route to external hosts, such as DNS servers or external websites.

```
$ traceroute 8.8.8.8

$ traceroute google.com
```

Combine 'ping' and 'traceroute'

Using both **ping** and **traceroute** provides a comprehensive view of network connectivity and path issues.

Start with 'ping'

Begin by pinging the target host to check basic connectivity and measure round-trip time.

```
$ ping -c 4 192.168.1.1

$ ping -c 4 8.8.8.8
```

Use "traceroute for Path Analysis

If **ping** reveals high latency or packet loss, use **traceroute** to identify where along the route the issue occurs.

```
$ traceroute 192.168.1.1

$ traceroute 8.8.8.8
```

Consider a scenario where users report slow network performance when accessing external resources. Follow the below steps to diagnose the issue:

- Ping External DNS Server

Check the connectivity and latency to an external DNS server.

```
$ ping -c 4 8.8.8.8
```

- Trace the Route to External DNS Server

Analyze the path to the external DNS server to identify any bottlenecks or delays.

```
$ traceroute 8.8.8.8
```

- Ping Internal Gateway

Verify the internal network performance by pinging the gateway.

```
$ ping -c 4 192.168.1.1
```

- Trace the Route to Internal Gateway

Check the path to the internal gateway for any issues.

```
$ traceroute 192.168.1.1
```

- Analyze Results

- If **ping** to the external DNS server shows high latency or packet loss, and **traceroute** reveals delays at specific hops, the issue may lie with an intermediate network device or the ISP.
- If internal **ping** and **traceroute** results are normal, the internal network is likely functioning correctly.

Both, **Ping** and **traceroute** diagnostics work together to help pinpoint the source and nature of network problems. As a result, issues may be more precisely identified and addressed, leading to AlphaProject's optimal network performance.

Monitoring Network Traffic with Wireshark

Before diving into Wireshark, we shall explore some common Linux commands for monitoring network traffic.

Linux Commands for Monitoring Traffic

Using 'ifconfig' and 'ip' Commands

The **ifconfig** and **ip** commands provide basic information about network interfaces and traffic statistics.

- View Interface Statistics with **ifconfig**:

```
$ ifconfig eth0
```

- Following is the sample output:

```
eth0: flags=4163<UP,BROADCAST,RUNNING,MULTICAST> mtu 1500

 inet 192.168.1.100 netmask 255.255.255.0 broadcast
192.168.1.255

 inet6 fe80::1e4d:7aff:fe0b:2b8d prefixlen 64 scopeid
0x20<link>

 ether 1c:4d:7a:0b:2b:8d txqueuelen 1000 (Ethernet)

 RX packets 105467 bytes 13245678 (12.6 MiB)

 RX errors 0 dropped 0 overruns 0 frame 0
```

```
 TX packets 104321 bytes 11456789 (10.9 MiB)
 TX errors 0 dropped 0 overruns 0 carrier 0 collisions 0
```

- View Interface Statistics with **ip**:

```
$ ip -s link show eth0
```

- Following is the sample output:

```
2: eth0: <BROADCAST,MULTICAST,UP,LOWER_UP> mtu 1500 qdisc pfifo_fast state UP mode DEFAULT group default qlen 1000
 link/ether 1c:4d:7a:0b:2b:8d brd ff:ff:ff:ff:ff:ff
 RX: bytes packets errors dropped overrun mcast
 13245678 105467 0 0 0 0
 TX: bytes packets errors dropped carrier collsns
 11456789 104321 0 0 0 0
```

Using 'netstat' Command

The **netstat** command displays network connections, routing tables, interface statistics, masquerade connections, and multicast memberships.

- View Active Connections:

```
$ netstat -tuln
```

- Following is the sample output:

```
Active Internet connections (only servers)
Proto Recv-Q Send-Q Local Address Foreign Address State
tcp 0 0 0.0.0.0:22 0.0.0.0:* LISTEN
```

```
tcp6 0 0 :::22 :::* LISTEN

udp 0 0 0.0.0.0:68 0.0.0.0:*

udp6 0 0 :::546 :::*
```

- View Interface Statistics:

```
$ netstat -i
```

- Following is the sample output:

```
Kernel Interface table

Iface MTU RX-OK RX-ERR RX-DRP RX-OVR TX-OK TX-ERR TX-DRP
TX-OVR Flg

eth0 1500 105467 0 0 0 104321 0 0 0 BMRU

lo 65536 45678 0 0 0 45678 0 0 0 LRU
```

Using 'ss' Command

The **ss** command is a modern replacement for **netstat** and provides more detailed information about socket connections.

- View Active Connections:

```
$ ss -tuln
```

- Following is the sample output:

```
Netid State Recv-Q Send-Q Local Address:Port Peer
Address:Port

tcp LISTEN 0 128 0.0.0.0:22 0.0.0.0:*

tcp LISTEN 0 128 [::]:22 [::]:*

udp UNCONN 0 0 0.0.0.0:68 0.0.0.0:*
```

```
udp UNCONN 0 0 [::]:546 [::]:*
```

Using 'iftop' Command

The **iftop** command provides a real-time bandwidth usage monitor.

- Install **iftop**:

```
$ sudo apt install iftop
```

- Run **iftop**:

```
$ sudo iftop -i eth0
```

- Following is the sample output:

```
Interface: eth0

Host name lookup enabled

Netlink MAC support enabled


 1.98Gb 3.96Gb 5.94Gb

---------------------------------------------------------
-------------------

192.168.1.100 => 192.168.1.1 1.92Kb 1.92Kb 1.92Kb

 <= 1.89Kb 1.89Kb 1.89Kb

---------------------------------------------------------
-------------------

Total send rate: 1.92Kb 1.92Kb 1.92Kb

Total receive rate: 1.89Kb 1.89Kb 1.89Kb
```

```
Total send and receive rate: 3.81Kb 3.81Kb 3.81Kb
```

Exploring Wireshark

Wireshark is an advanced network protocol analyzer that captures and displays data packets for in-depth assessment. It has a graphical user interface that makes it easy to understand network data and supports multiple protocols. A network packet analyzer is like a voltmeter for electrical cables; it measures current and voltage but at a higher level, allowing it to see what's going on inside a network cable.

These tools were either highly exclusive or prohibitively costly in earlier days. But that was before the release of Wireshark. Being both free and open source, Wireshark has quickly become one of the most popular and effective packet analyzers on the market.

Installing Wireshark

To install Wireshark on Ubuntu, use the following commands:

```
$ sudo apt update

$ sudo apt install wireshark
```

During the installation, you may be prompted to allow non-superusers to capture packets. Select 'Yes' and continue.

Adding Your User to the Wireshark Group

To allow your user to capture packets without root privileges, add your user to the **wireshark** group:

```
$ sudo usermod -aG wireshark $(whoami)
```

Log out and log back in for the changes to take effect.

Starting Wireshark

Launch Wireshark from the application menu or by typing the following command in the terminal:

```
$ wireshark
```

Capturing Packets with Wireshark

When Wireshark starts, you will see a list of available network interfaces. Follow these steps to start capturing packets:

- Select the desired network interface (e.g., **eth0**).
- Click the "Start" button to begin capturing packets.

Wireshark will start capturing packets on the selected interface and display them in real-time.

Filtering Captured Traffic

Wireshark allows you to apply filters to focus on specific types of traffic. Some common filters include:

- Filter by IP Address:

```
ip.addr == 192.168.1.1
```

- Filter by Protocol:

```
tcp

udp

icmp
```

- Filter by Port Number:

```
tcp.port == 80

udp.port == 53
```

Analyzing Packets and Saving Capture

Click on a packet in the capture window to view its details. The packet details pane displays information about the packet's layers, such as Ethernet, IP, TCP, and application layer protocols.

To save a capture for later analysis:

  - Click **File > Save As**.
  - Choose a location and file name, then click **Save**.

To load a saved capture:

  - Click **File > Open**.
  - Select the capture file and click **Open**.

Sample Program: Network Traffic Analysis using Wireshark

We shall now perform a network traffic analysis for AlphaProject using Wireshark.

Start Wireshark

Open Wireshark and select the network interface you want to monitor (e.g., **eth0**). Click "Start" to begin capturing packets.

Generate Network Traffic

To generate network traffic, you can use commands like **ping** and **curl**:

- Ping an External Host:

```
$ ping -c 4 google.com
```

- Fetch a Web Page:

```
$ curl -O http://gitforgits.com
```

Apply Filters in Wireshark

To focus on the traffic generated by the **ping** command, apply an ICMP filter:

- Type **icmp** in the filter bar and press Enter.

To focus on the HTTP traffic generated by the **curl** command, apply an HTTP filter:

- Type **http** in the filter bar and press Enter.

Analyze Packets and Save Capture

Click on a packet to view its details. For example, an ICMP packet will show the source and destination IP addresses, ICMP type, and code.

And now, save the capture for future reference:

- Click **File > Save As**.
- Choose a location and file name, then click **Save**.

Advanced Wireshark Features

Wireshark offers several advanced features for detailed network analysis:

Following TCP Streams

To follow a TCP stream, right-click on a TCP packet and select **Follow > TCP Stream**.

Wireshark will display the entire conversation between the client and server, making it easier to analyze data exchanges.

Using Display Filters

Display filters refine the view to show only specific packets. Some useful display filters include:

- Show HTTP Traffic:

```
http
```

- Show DNS Traffic:

```
dns
```

- Show ARP Traffic:

```
arp
```

- Show Traffic Between Two IPs:

```
ip.src == 192.168.1.100 && ip.dst == 192.168.1.200
```

Creating Custom Profiles

Wireshark allows you to create custom profiles with specific settings and filters:

- Click **Edit > Configuration Profiles > New**.
- Enter a profile name and configure the settings as needed.

Switch between profiles to quickly adapt Wireshark to different analysis scenarios.

Exporting Data

To export packet data for external analysis:

- Select the packets you want to export.
- Click **File > Export Packet Dissections > As Plain Text...**.
- Choose the format and options, then save the file.

Using Command Line Wireshark 'tshark'

Wireshark also provides a command-line interface called **tshark** for capturing and analyzing packets without a graphical interface.

- Capture Packets with **tshark**:

```
$ sudo tshark -i eth0 -w capture.pcap
```

- Apply Filters with **tshark**:

```
$ sudo tshark -r capture.pcap -Y "http"
```

Sample Program: Using Advanced Wireshark Capabilities

Follow a TCP Stream

Capture some HTTP traffic by fetching a web page:

```
$ curl -O http://gitforgits.com
```

In Wireshark, apply an HTTP filter:

```
http
```

Right-click on an HTTP packet and select **Follow > TCP Stream** to view the conversation.

Export HTTP Traffic

- Export the HTTP traffic for external analysis:
    - Apply the HTTP filter.
    - Select the packets.
    - Click **File > Export Packet Dissections > As Plain Text....**
- Choose a location and file name, then save the file.

Use 'tshark' for Command-Line Capture

- Capture packets using **tshark**:

```
$ sudo tshark -i eth0 -w alphaproject_capture.pcap
```

- Apply a filter to analyze the captured traffic:

```
$ sudo tshark -r alphaproject_capture.pcap -Y "http"
```

Deep network traffic analysis for AlphaProject is possible only with the help of Wireshark and its powerful advanced features. By this powerful means and in this way, you can keep an eye on how well your network is running, identify and fix problems, and guarantee that your network is stable and safe.

Troubleshooting Network Issues

Misconfigurations, malfunctioning hardware, outdated software, and external factors are just a few of the many potential causes of network problems. To effectively troubleshoot, one must first recognize the symptoms, then isolate the source of the problem, and finally implement solutions. In this section, we will go over some of the more typical network problems that could arise in AlphaProject and show you how to fix them with Linux tools.

Common Network Issues

1. Connectivity Problems:
    - Inability to reach internal or external hosts.
    - Dropped connections or intermittent connectivity.
2. IP Address Conflicts: Multiple devices assigned the same IP address.
3. DNS Resolution Failures: Inability to resolve domain names to IP addresses.
4. Slow Network Performance: High latency, packet loss, and slow data transfer rates.
5. Service Failures: Network services (e.g., DHCP, DNS, NFS) not functioning correctly.
6. Firewall Issues: Incorrect firewall rules blocking legitimate traffic.
7. Routing Problems: Incorrect or missing routes causing communication failures.
8. Security Incidents: Unauthorized access or network attacks.

Tools for Troubleshooting Network Issues

1. Ping: Tests connectivity to a host.
2. Traceroute: Traces the path packets take to a destination.
3. ifconfig/ip: Displays network interface configurations and statistics.
4. netstat/ss: Shows network connections and listening ports.
5. nslookup/dig: Troubleshoots DNS resolution issues.
6. Tcpdump: Captures and analyzes network packets.
7. Nmap: Scans for open ports and services.
8. Systemctl: Manages system services.
9. Journalctl: View system logs.

Connectivity Problems

Inability to Reach Internal or External Hosts

Use **ifconfig** or **ip** to verify that the network interfaces are up and configured correctly.

```
$ ip addr show eth0
```

Following is the sample output:

```
2: eth0: <BROADCAST,MULTICAST,UP,LOWER_UP> mtu 1500 qdisc
pfifo_fast state UP group default qlen 1000

 link/ether 1c:4d:7a:0b:2b:8d brd ff:ff:ff:ff:ff:ff

 inet 192.168.1.100/24 brd 192.168.1.255 scope global
eth0

 valid_lft forever preferred_lft forever

 inet6 fe80::1e4d:7aff:fe0b:2b8d/64 scope link

 valid_lft forever preferred_lft forever
```

Ensure the interface is UP and has a valid IP address. And, then ping the gateway to check connectivity within the local network.

```
$ ping -c 4 192.168.1.1
```

Following is the sample output:

```
PING 192.168.1.1 (192.168.1.1) 56(84) bytes of data.

64 bytes from 192.168.1.1: icmp_seq=1 ttl=64 time=0.234
ms

64 bytes from 192.168.1.1: icmp_seq=2 ttl=64 time=0.218
ms
```

```
64 bytes from 192.168.1.1: icmp_seq=3 ttl=64 time=0.211
ms
```

If the gateway is reachable, ping an external host.

```
$ ping -c 4 8.8.8.8
```

Use **traceroute** to identify where the connection fails.

```
$ traceroute 8.8.8.8
```

Following is the sample output:

```
traceroute to 8.8.8.8 (8.8.8.8), 30 hops max, 60 byte
packets

 1 192.168.1.1 (192.168.1.1) 0.123 ms 0.098 ms 0.089 ms

 2 10.0.0.1 (10.0.0.1) 0.234 ms 0.218 ms 0.211 ms

 3 * * *

 4 * * *
```

Identify thc hop where the route fails.

IP Address Conflicts

Multiple Devices Assigned the Same IP Address

Review the DHCP lease table to identify conflicts.

```
$ sudo cat /var/lib/dhcp/dhcpd.leases
```

Following is the sample output:

```
lease 192.168.1.100 {
```

```
 starts 5 2024/05/23 12:34:56;
 ends 5 2024/05/23 12:44:56;
 cltt 5 2024/05/23 12:34:56;
 binding state active;
 next binding state free;
 hardware ethernet 1c:4d:7a:0b:2b:8d;
 uid "\x01\x1c\x4d\x7a\x0b\x2b\x8d";
}
```

Look for duplicate entries and then, assign unique IP addresses to conflicting devices.

DNS Resolution Failures

Inability to Resolve Domain Names

Use **nslookup** to test DNS resolution.

```
$ nslookup google.com
```

Following is the sample output:

```
Server:        8.8.8.8
Address: 8.8.8.8#53
Non-authoritative answer:
Name:    google.com
Address: 142.250.72.78
```

Use **dig** for more detailed output.

```
$ dig google.com
```

Verify the DNS server settings in **/etc/resolv.conf**.

```
$ cat /etc/resolv.conf
```

Following is the sample output:

```
nameserver 8.8.8.8

nameserver 8.8.4.4
```

Ensure the DNS servers are correctly configured.

Slow Network Performance

High Latency and Packet Loss

Use **ping** to measure latency.

```
$ ping -c 10 google.com
```

Following is the sample output:

```
PING google.com (142.250.72.78) 56(84) bytes of data.

64 bytes from 142.250.72.78: icmp_seq=1 ttl=116 time=12.3
ms

64 bytes from 142.250.72.78: icmp_seq=2 ttl=116 time=11.7
ms

64 bytes from 142.250.72.78: icmp_seq=3 ttl=116 time=11.9
ms
```

Look for high round-trip times and packet loss. Then, use **iftop** to monitor real-time bandwidth usage.

```
$ sudo iftop -i eth0
```

Identify bandwidth hogs and high-traffic sources. Andthen, use **tcpdump** to capture and analyze network traffic with Wireshark.

```
$ sudo tcpdump -i eth0 -w traffic.pcap
```

Service Failures

Network Services Not Functioning Correctly

Verify the status of network services.

```
$ sudo systemctl status isc-dhcp-server

$ sudo systemctl status bind9

$ sudo systemctl status nfs-kernel-server
```

Ensure the services are active and running. Use **journalctl** to review service logs.

```
$ sudo journalctl -u isc-dhcp-server

$ sudo journalctl -u bind9

$ sudo journalctl -u nfs-kernel-server
```

Identify any error messages or issues. Restart the services if needed.

```
$ sudo systemctl restart isc-dhcp-server

$ sudo systemctl restart bind9

$ sudo systemctl restart nfs-kernel-server
```

Firewall Issues

Incorrect Firewall Rules Blocking Legitimate Traffic

List the current firewall rules using **iptables**.

```
$ sudo iptables -L -v -n
```

Following is the sample output:

```
Chain INPUT (policy ACCEPT 0 packets, 0 bytes)
 pkts bytes target prot opt in out source destination
 0 0 ACCEPT all -- lo * 0.0.0.0/0 0.0.0.0/0
 0 0 ACCEPT all -- eth0 * 192.168.1.0/24 0.0.0.0/0
 0 0 DROP all -- eth0 * 0.0.0.0/0 0.0.0.0/0
```

Adjust the firewall rules to allow legitimate traffic.

```
$ sudo iptables -A INPUT -p tcp --dport 80 -j ACCEPT
$ sudo iptables -A INPUT -p tcp --dport 443 -j ACCEPT
```

Save the firewall rules.

Routing Problems

Incorrect or Missing Routes

View the current routing table.

```
$ ip route show
```

Following is the sample output:

```
default via 192.168.1.1 dev eth0 proto static
192.168.1.0/24 dev eth0 proto kernel scope link src
192.168.1.100
```

Add any missing routes.

```
$ sudo ip route add 10.0.0.0/24 via 192.168.1.1
```

Verify the new route.

```
$ ip route show
```

Security Incidents

Unauthorized Access or Network Attacks

Review system logs for any suspicious activity with **journalctl.**

```
$ sudo journalctl -xe
```

Identify any unusual login attempts or security alerts. Scan for open ports and services.

```
$ sudo nmap -sS 192.168.1.100
```

Following is the sample output:

```
Starting Nmap 7.60 ( https://nmap.org ) at 2024-05-23
14:23 UTC

Nmap scan report for 192.168.1.100

Host is up (0.0010s latency).

Not shown: 996 closed ports

PORT STATE SERVICE

22/tcp open ssh

80/tcp open http

443/tcp open https
```

Identify any unexpected open ports. Capture and analyze network traffic for suspicious activity.

```
$ sudo tcpdump -i eth0 -w security.pcap
```

Analyze the captured traffic with Wireshark finally.

Sample Program: Troubleshooting Network Performance and Connectivity Issues in AlphaProject

Consider a scenario where users report slow network performance and intermittent connectivity issues within AlphaProject. Adopt the following steps to diagnose and troubleshoot the issues:

Verify Network Interface Status

Check the status of network interfaces.

```
$ ip addr show eth0
```

Ensure the interface is up and configured correctly.

Test Connectivity with 'ping'

Ping the gateway and external hosts to measure latency and packet loss.

```
$ ping -c 10 192.168.1.1

$ ping -c 10 8.8.8.8
```

Identify any high latency or packet loss.

Trace the Route with 'traceroute'

Trace the route to external hosts to identify where the connection fails.

```
$ traceroute 8.8.8.8
```

Locate any problematic hops.

Analyze Traffic with 'iftop'

Monitor real-time bandwidth usage.

```
$ sudo iftop -i eth0
```

Identify bandwidth hogs and high-traffic sources.

Capture Traffic with 'tcpdump'

Capture network traffic for detailed analysis.

```
$ sudo tcpdump -i eth0 -w traffic.pcap
```

Analyze the capture with Wireshark to identify any suspicious activity or anomalies.

Check Service Status with 'systemctl'

Verify the status of critical network services.

```
$ sudo systemctl status isc-dhcp-server

$ sudo systemctl status bind9

$ sudo systemctl status nfs-kernel-server
```

Ensure the services are active and running.

Review Logs with 'journalctl'

Check system logs for any error messages or issues.

```
$ sudo journalctl -u isc-dhcp-server

$ sudo journalctl -u bind9

$ sudo journalctl -u nfs-kernel-server
```

Identify and resolve any logged issues.

Adjust Firewall Rules

Ensure firewall rules are not blocking legitimate traffic.

```
$ sudo iptables -L -v -n
```

Modify rules if necessary.

```
$ sudo iptables -A INPUT -p tcp --dport 80 -j ACCEPT

$ sudo iptables -A INPUT -p tcp --dport 443 -j ACCEPT
```

Check Routing Table

Verify the routing table and add any missing routes.

```
$ ip route show

$ sudo ip route add 10.0.0.0/24 via 192.168.1.1
```

Monitor Security

Scan for open ports and analyze traffic for security incidents.

```
$ sudo nmap -sS 192.168.1.100

$ sudo tcpdump -i eth0 -w security.pcap
```

Review the captured traffic with Wireshark.

These above learned steps will walkthrough you through the process of using various Linux tools to efficiently diagnose network issues within AlphaProject. In addition to improving the overall performance and security of your network infrastructure, this also guarantees that your network operations will be smooth and dependable.

Managing Wireless Networks

Configuring and maintaining access points, switches, and routers is an important part of managing wireless networks. This helps to guarantee that the network connectivity is both seamless and scalable. This part will walk you through the steps of configuring key components, administering numerous activities connected to wireless networks, and scaling the current wireless networks of AlphaProject.

Scaling Wireless Networks

Scaling a wireless network involves expanding its capacity and coverage to support more devices and users. This process includes adding new access points, configuring switches, and ensuring that the network can handle increased traffic without performance degradation.

Assessing Current Network Capacity

Begin by assessing the current network capacity and identifying areas that require expansion. Use network monitoring tools to gather data on traffic patterns, device counts, and coverage gaps.

Adding New Access Points

- To scale the network, add new wireless access points (APs) to extend coverage and support more devices.
- Choose access points that support the required wireless standards (e.g., 802.11ac, 802.11ax) and have sufficient capacity for the expected number of devices.
- Physically install the new access points in strategic locations to ensure optimal coverage. Configure the access points using their management interface.
- Following is the sample configuration for Ubiquiti UniFi AP:
    - Access the UniFi Controller interface via a web browser.
    - Go to the "Devices" section and click "Adopt" next to the new access point.
    - Set the SSID (network name) and configure security settings (e.g., WPA2, WPA3).
    - Optimize the channels and transmit power to minimize interference.

Configuring Switches

- Configure network switches to handle increased traffic and ensure efficient data flow between wired and wireless devices.
- Access the switch management interface using a web browser or command-line tool.

Following is the sample configuration for Cisco Switch:

```
# Log in to the switch

ssh admin@switch_ip_address

# Enter global configuration mode

switch> enable

switch# configure terminal

# Configure VLAN for wireless network

switch(config)# vlan 10

switch(config-vlan)# name Wireless
```

```
switch(config-vlan)# exit


# Assign VLAN to switch ports connected to APs
switch(config)# interface gigabitethernet 0/1
switch(config-if)# switchport mode access
switch(config-if)# switchport access vlan 10
switch(config-if)# exit


# Save the configuration
switch(config)# end
switch# write memory
```

Ensuring Network Scalability

- Implement Quality of Service (QoS) policies and load balancing to ensure network scalability and performance.
- Prioritize network traffic to ensure that critical applications receive sufficient bandwidth.

Following is the sample QoS configuration:

```
# Log in to the switch
ssh admin@switch_ip_address


# Enter global configuration mode
switch> enable
switch# configure terminal
```

```
# Define QoS policy
switch(config)# class-map match-all HighPriority
switch(config-cmap)# match ip dscp 46
switch(config-cmap)# exit

switch(config)# policy-map QoSPolicy
switch(config-pmap)# class HighPriority
switch(config-pmap-c)# set dscp 46
switch(config-pmap)# exit

# Apply QoS policy to interface
switch(config)# interface gigabitethernet 0/1
switch(config-if)# service-policy input QoSPolicy
switch(config-if)# exit

# Save the configuration
switch(config)# end
switch# write memory
```

Configuring Access Points, Switches, and Routers

Proper configuration of access points, switches, and routers is crucial for maintaining a robust and secure wireless network.

Configuring Access Points

Log in to the access point's management interface using a web browser. Following is the sample configuration for TP-Link AP:

- Open a web browser and navigate to the AP's IP address.
- Go to the "Wireless" section and configure the SSID.
- Set up WPA2/WPA3 security.
- Adjust the channel and bandwidth settings to minimize interference.

Configuring Switches

Access the switch management interface via a web browser or command-line tool.

Following is the sample configuration for Netgear Switch:

```
# Log in to the switch

ssh admin@switch_ip_address


# Enter global configuration mode

switch> enable

switch# configure terminal


# Configure VLANs for wireless network

switch(config)# vlan 20

switch(config-vlan)# name Wireless

switch(config-vlan)# exit


# Assign VLAN to switch ports connected to APs

switch(config)# interface ethernet 0/2
```

```
switch(config-if)# switchport mode access
switch(config-if)# switchport access vlan 20
switch(config-if)# exit

# Save the configuration
switch(config)# end
switch# write memory
```

Configuring Routers

Log in to the router's management interface using a web browser. Following is the sample configuration for Cisco Router:

```
# Log in to the router
ssh admin@router_ip_address

# Enter global configuration mode
router> enable
router# configure terminal

# Configure wireless network
router(config)# interface wlan 0
router(config-if)# ssid AlphaProject
router(config-if)# encryption mode ciphers aes-ccm
```

```
router(config-if)# authentication open

router(config-if)# authentication key-management wpa
version 2

router(config-if)# wpa-psk ascii 0 your_password

router(config-if)# end


# Save the configuration

router# write memory
```

Monitoring Wireless Network Performance

Use tools like **iwconfig**, **iwlist**, and **iperf** to monitor and test wireless network performance. First, view the configuration and status of wireless interfaces with **iwconfig** as below:

```
$ iwconfig
```

Following is the sample output:

```
wlan0 IEEE 802.11bgn ESSID:"AlphaProject"

 Mode:Managed Frequency:2.437 GHz Access Point:
1C:4D:7A:0B:2B:8D

 Bit Rate=54 Mb/s Tx-Power=20 dBm

 Retry long limit:7 RTS thr=2347 B Fragment thr:off

 Power Management:off

 Link Quality=70/70 Signal level=-39 dBm Noise level=-92
dBm

 Rx invalid nwid:0 Rx invalid crypt:0 Rx invalid frag:0
```

```
Tx excessive retries:0 Invalid misc:0 Missed beacon:0
```

Then, List available wireless networks with **iwlist.**

```
$ sudo iwlist wlan0 scan
```

Following is the sample output:

```
wlan0 Scan completed :
 Cell 01 - Address: 1C:4D:7A:0B:2B:8D
 Channel:6
 Frequency:2.437 GHz (Channel 6)
 Quality=70/70 Signal level=-39 dBm
 Encryption key:on
 ESSID:"AlphaProject"
 Bit Rates:54 Mb/s; 48 Mb/s; 36 Mb/s; 24 Mb/s; 18 Mb/s;
12 Mb/s; 9 Mb/s; 6 Mb/s
 Mode:Master
 Extra:tsf=0000000000000000
 Extra: Last beacon: 10ms ago
 IE: Unknown: 000B416C70686150726F6A656374
```

Use **iperf** to test the network bandwidth between a client and server. At first, install **iperf** on Both Client and Server:

```
$ sudo apt install iperf
```

Run **iperf** Server:

```
$ iperf -s
```

Run **iperf** Client:

```
$ iperf -c server_ip_address
```

Following is the sample output:

```
------------------------------------------------------------
---

Client connecting to 192.168.1.100, TCP port 5001

TCP window size: 85.3 KByte (default)

------------------------------------------------------------
---

[ 3] local 192.168.1.101 port 5001 connected with
192.168.1.100 port 5001

[ ID] Interval Transfer Bandwidth

[ 3] 0.0-10.0 sec 112 MBytes 94.1 Mbits/sec
```

Securing Wireless Networks

Configure security settings to protect the wireless network from unauthorized access and potential threats. At first, ensure that access points and clients support WPA3 for enhanced security.

Following is the sample WPA3 configuration:

- Log in to the AP Management Interface: Open a web browser and navigate to the AP's IP address.
- Configure WPA3 Security: Go to the "Wireless Security" section and select WPA3. Set the passphrase and apply the settings.

Then, allow only specific devices to connect to the wireless network by configuring MAC address filtering. Following is the sample configuration:

- Open a web browser and navigate to the AP's IP address.

- Go to the "MAC Filtering" section and add the MAC addresses of allowed devices.

Managing Wireless Network Settings

Regularly update firmware and configurations to ensure optimal performance and security.

First, check for firmware updates and apply them to access points, switches, and routers.

Following is the sample firmware update for TP-Link AP:

- Open a web browser and navigate to the AP's IP address.
- Go to the "Firmware" section and check for available updates.
- Download and apply the update.

Then, create backups of the current configurations to restore them if needed, with following code snippet:

```
# Log in to the router

ssh admin@router_ip_address


# Enter privileged EXEC mode

router> enable


# Backup configuration

router# copy running-config startup-config


# Restore configuration

router# copy startup-config running-config
```

To summarize, the process includes setting up the network's hardware, including access points, switches, and routers; keeping tabs on how well the network is doing; and putting safeguards in place. Following these procedures will assist in keeping a wireless network architecture strong enough to manage the requirements of contemporary IT settings.

Summary

This chapter covered a lot of momentum of this book in terms of network management, with an emphasis on how to put theory into practice and fix common problems. The chapter started out by going over the various kinds of network interfaces, including Ethernet, wireless, loopback, and virtual interfaces. Specifically, it covered the ins and outs of configuring IP addresses and routing for efficient internal and external communication. We showed how to manage network services, including how to configure and set up DHCP, DNS, and NFS, so that everything runs well and everyone can share the resources.

Examples utilizing ping and traceroute to detect and fix connectivity problems brought attention to the significance of network diagnosis. There was an introduction to Wireshark, an application for monitoring network traffic, and instructions on how to set it up and use it for in-depth analysis. Using a variety of Linux commands and tools, the chapter addressed typical network problems and their remedies, including connectivity issues, IP address disputes, DNS resolution errors, and sluggish network performance.

In addition, the chapter covered how to manage wireless networks, including how to scale up or down current wireless equipment, set up access points, switches, and routers, and keep tabs on how well your network is doing with tools like iwconfig, iwlist, and iperf. Methods for making sure the network can grow were also learned, including load balancing and quality of service regulations.

Chapter 3: Security and Monitoring

Introduction

In Chapter 3, "Security and Monitoring," you will explore the critical aspects of safeguarding and monitoring your Linux systems. This chapter begins with an exploration of **`iptables`** and **`firewalld`**, providing insights into configuring firewalls to protect your network from unauthorized access and potential threats. You will learn how to implement AppArmor, a security module that enhances system security by enforcing access controls.

The chapter covers performing security audits with Lynis, a tool that evaluates system security and suggests improvements. You will also understand the importance of periodical security updates and patching to keep your systems secure against vulnerabilities. Monitoring system logs for security is another essential aspect you will explore, learning how to identify and respond to security incidents.

An introduction to Snort will help you understand its role in network intrusion detection and prevention. You will learn how to use Intrusion Detection Systems (IDS) to monitor and analyze network traffic for suspicious activities. Securing SSH access is crucial for maintaining secure remote connections, and this chapter provides practical steps to enhance SSH security. Additionally, configuring VPNs for secure connections ensures data protection during transmission over untrusted networks. Finally, you will learn about managing certificates and encryption to secure communications and protect sensitive information.

By the end of this chapter, you will be equipped with the knowledge and skills to implement robust security measures and monitor your Linux systems effectively, ensuring a secure and resilient IT environment for AlphaProject.

Exploring 'iptables' and 'firewalld'

Introduction to 'iptables'

`iptables` is a command-line utility in Linux used to configure the IPv4 packet filtering rules of the Linux kernel's netfilter framework. It allows administrators to define rules for how incoming, outgoing, and forwarded packets should be handled by the system, providing a powerful means of implementing security policies and controlling network traffic.

Key Purposes of 'iptables'

1. Packet Filtering: Controls which packets are allowed or denied based on defined rules.
2. Network Address Translation (NAT): Modifies packet headers for IP masquerading or port forwarding.
3. Logging: Tracks and logs packets that match certain criteria for monitoring and troubleshooting.
4. Stateful Inspection: Maintains the state of active connections and makes decisions based

on connection state.

Benefits of 'iptables'

- Allows detailed control over network traffic based on IP addresses, ports, protocols, and connection states.
- Can be configured to handle complex scenarios and specific security requirements.
- Works closely with other system components, providing a comprehensive security framework.

Introduction to 'firewalld'

`firewalld` is a dynamic firewall management tool with support for network/firewall zones that define the trust level of network connections or interfaces. It uses **`iptables`** in the background but provides a more user-friendly interface for managing firewall rules.

Key Purposes of 'firewalld'

1. Dynamic Rule Management: Allows for changes to the firewall configuration without interrupting existing connections.
2. Zone-Based Configuration: Uses zones to define the trust level of network interfaces, simplifying management of complex firewall rules.
3. Service Management: Provides predefined services, making it easier to allow or block traffic based on common use cases.
4. IPv4, IPv6, and NAT Support: Handles various protocols and network address translation requirements seamlessly.

Benefits of 'firewalld'

- Ease of Use: Simplifies the management of firewall rules with a higher-level abstraction than **iptables**.
- Dynamic Capabilities: Enables changes to be made on the fly without restarting the firewall.
- Zone Concept: Helps manage different trust levels for different network interfaces or connections.

'iptables' Syntax and Commands

`iptables` uses tables, chains, and rules to manage network traffic. Tables define the rule sets, chains are lists of rules, and rules specify the conditions under which packets are matched and actions are taken.

Tables in 'iptables'

1. filter: The default table for filtering packets. Contains chains like INPUT, FORWARD,

and OUTPUT.

2. nat: Handles Network Address Translation. Contains chains like PREROUTING, POSTROUTING, and OUTPUT.
3. mangle: Used for specialized packet alteration. Contains chains like PREROUTING, POSTROUTING, INPUT, OUTPUT, and FORWARD.
4. raw: Primarily used for configuring exemptions from connection tracking. Contains PREROUTING and OUTPUT chains.

Chains in 'iptables'

- INPUT: Handles incoming packets destined for the local system.
- FORWARD: Manages packets being routed through the system.
- OUTPUT: Deals with packets generated locally and leaving the system.
- PREROUTING: Alters packets as soon as they come in.
- POSTROUTING: Alters packets before they leave.

Basic 'iptables' Commands

1. List Rules:
   - **iptables -L**: Lists all current rules.
   - **iptables -L -v**: Provides a verbose listing with packet counts and byte counts.
2. Add a Rule:
   - **iptables -A <chain> -p <protocol> --dport <port> -j <target>**: Appends a rule to a specified chain.
3. Delete a Rule:
   - **iptables -D <chain> <rule_number>**: Deletes a specific rule from a chain.
4. Insert a Rule:
   - **iptables -I <chain> <rule_number> -p <protocol> --dport <port> -j <target>**: Inserts a rule at a specific position in a chain.
5. Flush Rules:
   - **iptables -F**: Flushes all rules in all chains.
   - **iptables -F <chain>**: Flushes all rules in a specified chain.
6. Save and Restore Rules:
   - **iptables-save > /path/to/file**: Saves the current rules to a file.
   - **iptables-restore < /path/to/file**: Restores rules from a file.

Targets in 'iptables'

- ACCEPT: Allows the packet to pass.
- DROP: Discards the packet without any response.
- REJECT: Discards the packet and sends an appropriate response to the sender.
- LOG: Logs the packet details to the system log.

‘firewalld’ Syntax and Commands

firewalld simplifies firewall management by using zones and predefined services. Zones define the trust level for network interfaces, and services define sets of rules for common applications.

Zones in ‘firewalld’

1. Drop: Any incoming network packets are dropped, with no reply.
2. Block: Any incoming network connections are rejected with an icmp-host-prohibited message.
3. Public: For use in untrusted public areas. You do not trust other computers but can allow selected incoming connections.
4. External: For use on external networks with masquerading enabled.
5. Internal: For use on internal networks where you mostly trust the other computers on the networks.
6. DMZ: For computers in your demilitarized zone that are publicly accessible with limited access to your internal network.
7. Work: For use in work areas. You mostly trust the other computers on the networks.
8. Home: For use in home areas. You mostly trust the other computers on the networks.
9. Trusted: All network connections are accepted.

Basic ‘firewalld’ Commands

1. Starting and Stopping **firewalld**:
    - **sudo systemctl start firewalld**: Starts the **firewalld** service.
    - **sudo systemctl stop firewalld**: Stops the **firewalld** service.
    - **sudo systemctl enable firewalld**: Enables **firewalld** to start on boot.
    - **sudo systemctl disable firewalld**: Disables **firewalld** from starting on boot.
2. Checking Status:
    - **sudo firewall-cmd --state**: Checks the current state of **firewalld**.
    - **sudo firewall-cmd --get-active-zones**: Lists the active zones.
3. Managing Zones:
    - **sudo firewall-cmd --get-zones**: Lists all available zones.
    - **sudo firewall-cmd --zone=<zone> --add-interface=<interface>**: Assigns a network interface to a zone.
    - **sudo firewall-cmd --zone=<zone> --remove-interface=<interface>**: Removes a network interface from a zone.
4. Managing Services:
    - **sudo firewall-cmd --zone=<zone> --add-service=<service>**: Adds a service to a zone.
    - **sudo firewall-cmd --zone=<zone> --remove-service=<service>**: Removes a

service from a zone.
    - **sudo firewall-cmd --zone=<zone> --list-services**: Lists all services allowed in a zone.
5. Managing Ports:
    - **sudo firewall-cmd --zone=<zone> --add-port=<port>/tcp**: Opens a port for TCP traffic.
    - **sudo firewall-cmd --zone=<zone> --remove-port=<port>/tcp**: Closes a port for TCP traffic.
    - **sudo firewall-cmd --zone=<zone> --list-ports**: Lists all open ports in a zone.
6. Making Changes Permanent:
    - **sudo firewall-cmd --runtime-to-permanent**: Converts runtime configurations to permanent configurations.
7. Reloading Configuration:
    - **sudo firewall-cmd --reload**: Reloads the firewall configuration to apply changes.

Administrators who understand **`iptables`** and **`firewalld`** may effectively control network traffic, enforce security policies, and protect the safety and integrity of their network environments. For managing AlphaProject's security and keeping a comprehensive firewall setup up and running, this expertise is crucial.

Configuring Firewalls

The configuration of firewalls is a crucial task for securing your network because it allows you to regulate the traffic that is coming into and going out of your network based on the security rules that you have already established. Continuing on the last section's introduction to **`iptables`** and **`firewalld`**, this section will show how to configure firewalls in the context of AlphaProject.

Following are the tasks Involved in Configuring Firewalls:

- Establish rules to allow or block traffic based on IP addresses, ports, and protocols.
- Assign network interfaces to specific zones with varying levels of trust.
- Set up rules for translating private IP addresses to public IP addresses.
- Implement logging to monitor traffic and troubleshoot issues.
- Ensure that the firewall rules are working as expected without disrupting legitimate traffic.

Configuring 'iptables' for AlphaProject

We shall configure **`iptables`** to secure the AlphaProject network by defining some following basic rules:

Allow SSH Access

To allow SSH access on port 22, add the following rule:

```
$ sudo iptables -A INPUT -p tcp --dport 22 -j ACCEPT
```

Allow HTTP and HTTPS Traffic

To allow HTTP and HTTPS traffic on ports 80 and 443, add these rules:

```
$ sudo iptables -A INPUT -p tcp --dport 80 -j ACCEPT

$ sudo iptables -A INPUT -p tcp --dport 443 -j ACCEPT
```

Allow Localhost Traffic

Allow all traffic on the loopback interface (**lo**):

```
$ sudo iptables -A INPUT -i lo -j ACCEPT
```

Drop All Other Incoming Traffic

To drop all other incoming traffic, add a default deny rule at the end:

```
$ sudo iptables -P INPUT DROP

$ sudo iptables -A INPUT -j DROP
```

Save and Restore 'iptables' Rules

To save the current **iptables** rules so they persist after a reboot, use the **iptables-save** command:

```
$ sudo iptables-save > /etc/iptables/rules.v4
```

To restore the rules, use the **iptables-restore** command:

```
$ sudo iptables-restore < /etc/iptables/rules.v4
```

Configuring 'firewalld' for AlphaProject

Now we shall configure **firewalld** to secure the AlphaProject network. We will use zones to define trust levels and assign interfaces accordingly as below:

Start and Enable firewalld

Ensure that **firewalld** is running and enabled to start at boot:

```
$ sudo systemctl start firewalld

$ sudo systemctl enable firewalld
```

Check the Default Zone

Check the default zone for new connections and interfaces:

```
$ sudo firewall-cmd --get-default-zone
```

Assign Interface to a Zone

Assign the **eth0** interface to the **public** zone:

```
$ sudo firewall-cmd --zone=public --change-interface=eth0
--permanent
```

Allow SSH Access

To allow SSH access in the **public** zone:

```
$ sudo firewall-cmd --zone=public --add-service=ssh --
permanent
```

Allow HTTP and HTTPS Traffic

To allow HTTP and HTTPS traffic in the **public** zone:

```
$ sudo firewall-cmd --zone=public --add-service=http --
permanent
```

```
$ sudo firewall-cmd --zone=public --add-service=https --
permanent
```

Allow Localhost Traffic

By default, **firewalld** allows all traffic on the loopback interface. Verify this configuration:

```
$ sudo firewall-cmd --zone=trusted --list-all
```

Reload Firewall Rules

Reload the firewall rules to apply the changes:

```
$ sudo firewall-cmd --reload
```

Verify the Configuration

List the rules in the **public** zone to verify the configuration:

```
$ sudo firewall-cmd --zone=public --list-all
```

Following is the sample output:

```
public (active)
 target: default
 icmp-block-inversion: no
 interfaces: eth0
 sources:
 services: dhcpv6-client http https ssh
 ports:
 protocols:
 masquerade: no
```

```
forward-ports:

source-ports:

icmp-blocks:

rich rules:
```

Sample Program: Firewall Configuration for AlphaProject

We shall implement a far better and a comprehensive firewall configuration for AlphaProject, covering both **iptables** and **firewalld**.

Configuring 'iptables' for AlphaProject

Allow Incoming SSH, HTTP, and HTTPS Traffic

```
$ sudo iptables -A INPUT -p tcp --dport 22 -j ACCEPT

$ sudo iptables -A INPUT -p tcp --dport 80 -j ACCEPT

$ sudo iptables -A INPUT -p tcp --dport 443 -j ACCEPT
```

Allow Established and Related Connections

```
$ sudo iptables -A INPUT -m conntrack --ctstate
ESTABLISHED,RELATED -j ACCEPT
```

Allow Loopback Traffic

```
$ sudo iptables -A INPUT -i lo -j ACCEPT
```

Log and Drop Other Incoming Traffic

```
$ sudo iptables -A INPUT -j LOG --log-prefix "iptables-
dropped: "

$ sudo iptables -A INPUT -j DROP
```

By default, **iptables** allows all outgoing traffic. Ensure this with:

```
$ sudo iptables -P OUTPUT ACCEPT
```

Save the Configuration

```
$ sudo iptables-save > /etc/iptables/rules.v4
```

Configuring 'firewalld' for AlphaProject

Start and Enable **firewalld**

```
$ sudo systemctl start firewalld

$ sudo systemctl enable firewalld
```

Set the default zone to **public**:

```
$ sudo firewall-cmd --set-default-zone=public
```

Assign Interface to **public** Zone

```
$ sudo firewall-cmd --zone=public --change-interface=eth0
--permanent
```

Allow SSH, HTTP, and HTTPS Services

```
$ sudo firewall-cmd --zone=public --add-service=ssh --
permanent

$ sudo firewall-cmd --zone=public --add-service=http --
permanent

$ sudo firewall-cmd --zone=public --add-service=https --
permanent
```

Add a rich rule to allow established and related connections:

```
$ sudo firewall-cmd --zone=public --add-rich-rule='rule
family="ipv4" service name="ssh" accept' --permanent

$ sudo firewall-cmd --zone=public --add-rich-rule='rule
family="ipv4" service name="http" accept' --permanent

$ sudo firewall-cmd --zone=public --add-rich-rule='rule
family="ipv4" service name="https" accept' --permanent
```

Add a rule to log and drop other incoming traffic:

```
$ sudo firewall-cmd --zone=public --add-rich-rule='rule
family="ipv4" log prefix="firewalld-dropped: "
level="info" drop' --permanent
```

By default, **firewalld** allows all outgoing traffic. Verify this configuration:

```
$ sudo firewall-cmd --zone=public --list-all
```

Reload the firewall rules to apply the changes:

```
$ sudo firewall-cmd --reload
```

List the rules in the **public** zone to verify the configuration:

```
$ sudo firewall-cmd --zone=public --list-all
```

Following is the sample output:

```
public (active)
  target: default
  icmp-block-inversion: no
  interfaces: eth0
```

```
sources:
services: ssh http https
ports:
protocols:
masquerade: no
forward-ports:
source-ports:
icmp-blocks:
rich rules:
rule family="ipv4" service name="ssh" accept
rule family="ipv4" service name="http" accept
rule family="ipv4" service name="https" accept
rule family="ipv4" log prefix="firewalld-dropped: "
level="info" drop
```

If you follow the above steps, you may set up firewalld and iptables to protect the AlphaProject network. This configuration provides a strong security framework for your network by allowing only authorized traffic and logging and dropping all other traffic.

Implementing AppArmor

Introduction to AppArmor

AppArmor (Application Armor) is a Linux Security Module (LSM) that provides a mechanism for limiting the capabilities of programs by confining them to a set of predefined rules. AppArmor enhances system security by enforcing access control policies on applications, thus preventing them from accessing resources they are not explicitly allowed to use.

AppArmor uses profiles to restrict the capabilities of applications. These profiles specify the resources that an application can access, such as files, directories, network sockets, and other system resources. By defining and enforcing these profiles, AppArmor helps in minimizing the risk of security breaches by confining applications to their intended operations.

Key Purposes of AppArmor:

1. Define roles and assign permissions to users and applications.
2. Create and enforce security policies to restrict application behavior.
3. Enhance user authentication and access control using Pluggable Authentication Modules (PAM).
4. Limit the resources that virtual machines can access.
5. Control the access of web applications to system resources.

Installing and Enabling AppArmor

Before implementing AppArmor, ensure it is installed and enabled on your system.

Install AppArmor

On Ubuntu, you can install AppArmor and its utilities using the following command:

```
$ sudo apt update

$ sudo apt install apparmor apparmor-utils
```

Enable AppArmor

Ensure that AppArmor is enabled and running:

```
$ sudo systemctl enable apparmor

$ sudo systemctl start apparmor
```

Verify the status of AppArmor:

```
$ sudo apparmor_status
```

Following is the sample output:

```
apparmor module is loaded.

40 profiles are loaded.
```

```
40 profiles are in enforce mode.
0 profiles are in complain mode.
2 processes have profiles defined.
2 processes are in enforce mode.
0 processes are in complain mode.
0 processes are unconfined but have a profile defined.
```

Defining and Enforcing AppArmor Policies

AppArmor profiles define the security policies for applications. These profiles can be created manually or generated using tools provided by AppArmor.

Create a Profile for a Specific Application

We shall create a profile for a sample application, **example-app**. First, locate the application binary:

```
$ which example-app
```

Assuming the application is located at **/usr/bin/example-app**, create a profile for it:

```
$ sudo aa-genprof /usr/bin/example-app
```

This command will start the AppArmor profiling mode, where you can define the policy interactively.

Define the Profile

Run the application to generate log entries:

```
$ sudo /usr/bin/example-app
```

AppArmor will monitor the application's behavior and generate profile entries. After running the application, finish the profile generation:

```
$ sudo aa-logprof
```

Follow the prompts to define the permissions for the application. Once done, the profile will be enforced.

Enforce the Profile

Ensure that the profile is enforced:

```
$ sudo aa-enforce /etc/apparmor.d/usr.bin.example-app
```

Verify the profile status:

```
$ sudo apparmor_status
```

Role-Based Access Control (RBAC)

AppArmor supports RBAC, allowing you to define roles and assign permissions to users and applications.

Define roles and assign permissions using AppArmor profiles. For example, create a profile for a web server role:

```
/etc/apparmor.d/usr.sbin.apache2
```

Edit the profile to define the permissions:

```
# Include common includes for apache2

#include <tunables/global>


/usr/sbin/apache2 {

 # Enforce read-only access to the web directory

 /var/www/html/ r,
```

```
 # Allow apache to read configuration files
 /etc/apache2/** r,

 # Allow apache to write to log files
 /var/log/apache2/** rw,

 # Deny access to any other files or directories
 deny /home/** rw,
 deny /etc/** rw,
}
```

Apply and enforce the role:

```
$ sudo aa-enforce /etc/apparmor.d/usr.sbin.apache2
```

Integrating AppArmor with PAM

AppArmor can be integrated with PAM to enhance user authentication and access control. Edit the PAM configuration file for SSH, typically located at **/etc/pam.d/sshd**:

```
$ sudo nano /etc/pam.d/sshd
```

Add the following line to integrate AppArmor:

```
auth required pam_apparmor.so
```

Create a profile for PAM modules, such as **/etc/apparmor.d/usr.sbin.sshd**, to define access control policies for SSH sessions.

```
# Include common includes for sshd
```

```
#include <tunables/global>


/usr/sbin/sshd {
 # Allow read access to SSH configuration files
 /etc/ssh/sshd_config r,

 # Allow sshd to execute its binary
 /usr/sbin/sshd ix,


 # Deny access to other sensitive files
 deny /etc/passwd rw,
 deny /etc/shadow rw,
}
```

Enforce the profile:

```
$ sudo aa-enforce /etc/apparmor.d/usr.sbin.sshd
```

Confining Virtual Machines

AppArmor can confine virtual machines, limiting their access to system resources. For example, create a profile for **`libvirtd`**, the daemon that manages virtual machines:

```
$ sudo aa-genprof /usr/sbin/libvirtd
```

Run the virtual machine manager to generate log entries:

```
$ sudo /usr/sbin/libvirtd
```

Complete the profile generation:

```
$ sudo aa-logprof
```

Edit the profile to define the permissions for virtual machines:

```
# Include common includes for libvirtd
#include <tunables/global>


/usr/sbin/libvirtd {
 # Allow libvirtd to read configuration files
 /etc/libvirt/** r,


 # Allow libvirtd to manage virtual machine images
 /var/lib/libvirt/images/** rwk,


 # Deny access to sensitive files
 deny /etc/passwd rw,
 deny /etc/shadow rw,
}
```

Enforce the profile:

```
$ sudo aa-enforce /etc/apparmor.d/usr.sbin.libvirtd
```

Restricting outside Web Apps

Restricting the access of web applications to system resources can enhance security. Create a profile for a web application, such as **/usr/bin/webapp**:

```
$ sudo aa-genprof /usr/bin/webapp
```

Run the web application to generate log entries:

```
$ sudo /usr/bin/webapp
```

Complete the profile generation:

```
$ sudo aa-logprof
```

Edit the profile to restrict the web application's access:

```
# Include common includes for webapp
#include <tunables/global>


/usr/bin/webapp {
  # Allow read-only access to the web directory
  /var/www/html/ r,


  # Deny access to sensitive directories
  deny /home/** rw,
  deny /etc/** rw,
  deny /var/log/** rw,
}
```

Enforce the profile:

```
$ sudo aa-enforce /etc/apparmor.d/usr.bin.webapp
```

Sample Program: Implementing AppArmor in AlphaProject

We shall implement AppArmor for AlphaProject by creating and enforcing profiles for different components.

To begin with, create a profile for the Apache web server:

```
$ sudo aa-genprof /usr/sbin/apache2
```

Run the Apache server to generate log entries:

```
$ sudo systemctl restart apache2
```

Complete the profile generation:

```
$ sudo aa-logprof
```

Edit the profile to define the permissions:

```
# Include common includes for apache2

#include <tunables/global>



/usr/sbin/apache2 {

 # Enforce read-only access to the web directory

 /var/www/html/ r,



 # Allow apache to read configuration files

 /etc/apache2/** r,
```

```
 # Allow apache to write to log files
 /var/log/apache2/** rw,

 # Deny access to any other files or directories
 deny /home/** rw,
 deny /etc/** rw,
}
```

Enforce the profile:

```
$ sudo aa-enforce /etc/apparmor.d/usr.sbin.apache2
```

Edit the PAM configuration file for SSH:

```
$ sudo nano /etc/pam.d/sshd
```

Add the following line:

```
auth required pam_apparmor.so
```

Create a profile for the SSH daemon:

```
/etc/apparmor.d/usr.sbin.sshd
```

Edit the profile:

```
# Include common includes for sshd
#include <tunables/global>
```

```
/usr/sbin/sshd {
 # Allow read access to SSH configuration files
 /etc/ssh/sshd_config r,

 # Allow sshd to execute its binary
 /usr/sbin/sshd ix,

 # Deny access to other sensitive files
 deny /etc/passwd rw,
 deny /etc/shadow rw,
}
```

Enforce the profile:

```
$ sudo aa-enforce /etc/apparmor.d/usr.sbin.sshd
```

Confine Virtual Machines

Create a profile for **libvirtd**:

```
$ sudo aa-genprof /usr/sbin/libvirtd
```

Run the virtual machine manager:

```
$ sudo /usr/sbin/libvirtd
```

Complete the profile generation:

```
$ sudo aa-logprof
```

Define permissions for virtual machines:

```
# Include common includes for libvirtd
#include <tunables/global>

/usr/sbin/libvirtd {
 # Allow libvirtd to read configuration files
 /etc/libvirt/** r,

 # Allow libvirtd to manage virtual machine images
 /var/lib/libvirt/images/** rwk,

 # Deny access to sensitive files
 deny /etc/passwd rw,
 deny /etc/shadow rw,
}
```

Enforce the profile:

```
$ sudo aa-enforce /etc/apparmor.d/usr.sbin.libvirtd
```

Restrict Outside Web Apps

Create a profile for the web application:

```
$ sudo aa-genprof /usr/bin/webapp
```

Run the web application:

```
$ sudo /usr/bin/webapp
```

Complete the profile generation:

```
$ sudo aa-logprof
```

Define permissions for the web application:

```
# Include common includes for webapp

#include <tunables/global>


/usr/bin/webapp {

  # Allow read-only access to the web directory

  /var/www/html/ r,


  # Deny access to sensitive directories

  deny /home/** rw,

  deny /etc/** rw,

  deny /var/log/** rw,

}
```

Enforce the profile:

```
$ sudo aa-enforce /etc/apparmor.d/usr.bin.webapp
```

By taking this method, the risk of unwanted access is effectively reduced, and it is ensured that apps function inside the bounds that were intended for them.

Performing Security Audits with Lynis

Introduction to Lynis

Lynis is an open-source security auditing tool designed for Unix-based systems. It searches the system thoroughly for vulnerabilities and suggests ways to strengthen it. Lynis is used to audit the security posture of Unix-based systems, including Linux, macOS, and BSD variants.

An integral aspect of keeping AlphaProject secure is Lynis, which is better for finding vulnerabilities, hardening systems, and doing compliance testing. It helps administrators by providing detailed insights into potential vulnerabilities and misconfigurations. Lynis covers various aspects of system security, including file permissions, firewall configurations, and installed software.

Key Features of Lynis:

1. Performs comprehensive security checks.
2. Evaluates system compliance with industry standards.
3. Provides recommendations for improving system security.
4. Identifies potential vulnerabilities and misconfigurations.

Installing Lynis

To use Lynis for security audits, you first need to install it on your system.

Install Lynis

You can install Lynis using the package manager:

```
$ sudo apt update

$ sudo apt install lynis
```

Alternatively, you can download the latest version from the official Lynis website and install it manually:

```
$ wget https://downloads.cisofy.com/lynis/lynis-
3.0.6.tar.gz

$ tar xzf lynis-3.0.6.tar.gz

$ cd lynis
```

Verify Installation

Verify that Lynis is installed correctly by running the following command:

```
$ sudo lynis show version
```

You should see the output indicating the version of Lynis installed.

Performing Security Audits with Lynis

Lynis can be used to perform a comprehensive security audit on the AlphaProject system.

Run a Basic Security Audit

To run a basic security audit, execute the following command:

```
$ sudo lynis audit system
```

This command will start a full system audit, covering various security aspects. Lynis will display the progress of the audit and provide detailed results at the end.

Analyze Audit Results

After the audit completes, Lynis will display a summary of the findings, including warnings, suggestions, and compliance scores. Review the results to identify critical issues and areas for improvement.

Following is the sample output:

```
Lynis security scan details:



Hardening index : 70 [############## ]

Tests performed: 260

Plugins enabled : 1



----------------------------
```

```
Warnings (8):

----------------------------

! Some important tests are missing

 (2017) Enable firewall

 (2018) No legal banner configured

 (2024) Test missing

Suggestions (14):

----------------------------

* Install a firewall

 (2017) Enable firewall

* Configure a legal banner

 (2018) No legal banner configured

...
```

Compliance Testing with Lynis

Lynis includes several compliance tests to ensure that your system meets industry standards and best practices.

Run Compliance Tests

To run compliance tests, use the following command:

```
$ sudo lynis audit system --compliance
```

This command will perform checks related to compliance standards, such as PCI-DSS, HIPAA, and CIS benchmarks. Lynis will provide a detailed report on the compliance status of your system.

Review Compliance Report

Review the compliance report generated by Lynis. The report will highlight areas where your system meets or fails to meet compliance requirements. Address any issues identified to improve compliance.

Following is the sample output:

```
Compliance status:

PCI-DSS: 75%

HIPAA: 80%

CIS: 70%
```

System Hardening with Lynis

Lynis provides recommendations for hardening your system based on the audit results. These recommendations help improve the overall security posture of your system as follows:

Identify Hardening Suggestions

After running a system audit, Lynis will provide a list of hardening suggestions. These suggestions are tailored to your system's configuration and highlight areas that need improvement.

Implement Hardening Measures

Review the hardening suggestions and implement the recommended measures. Some common hardening tasks include:

- Ensure that a firewall is configured and active.
- Restrict file permissions to prevent unauthorized access.
- Implement measures such as disabling root login and using key-based authentication.

Following is an example to harden/disable root login in SSH:

```
$ sudo nano /etc/ssh/sshd_config
```

Change the following line:

```
PermitRootLogin no
```

Restart the SSH service to apply the changes:

```
$ sudo systemctl restart sshd
```

Detecting Vulnerabilities with Lynis

Lynis helps in detecting potential vulnerabilities and misconfigurations that could compromise the security of your system.

Scan for Vulnerabilities

Run a security audit to scan for vulnerabilities:

```
$ sudo lynis audit system
```

Lynis will identify vulnerabilities and provide recommendations for mitigating them.

Address Identified Vulnerabilities

Review the audit report and address any identified vulnerabilities. This may involve updating software packages, modifying configurations, or applying patches.

```
$ sudo apt update
$ sudo apt upgrade
```

Sample Program: Implementing Lynis

We shall perform a comprehensive security audit for AlphaProject using Lynis, including compliance testing, system hardening, and vulnerability detection.

Run a Full System Audit

- Start by running a full system audit:

```
$ sudo lynis audit system
```

- After that, analyze the audit results to identify warnings, suggestions, and compliance scores and while doing so, note the critical issues that need immediate attention.

Perform Compliance Testing

- Run compliance tests to evaluate the system's adherence to industry standards:

```
$ sudo lynis audit system --compliance
```

- Review the compliance report and take note of any areas where the system fails to meet compliance requirements.

Implement Hardening Measures

Based on the audit and compliance results, implement the recommended hardening measures. This may include:

- Enabling a Firewall:

```
$ sudo apt install ufw

$ sudo ufw enable

$ sudo ufw allow ssh

$ sudo ufw allow http

$ sudo ufw allow https
```

- Securing SSH Access:

```
$ sudo nano /etc/ssh/sshd_config
```

- Modify the following lines:

```
PermitRootLogin no
```

```
PasswordAuthentication no
```

- Restart the SSH service:

```
$ sudo systemctl restart sshd
```

Scan for Vulnerabilities

- Run a security audit to identify vulnerabilities:

```
$ sudo lynis audit system
```

- After running it, address any identified vulnerabilities by updating software packages and modifying configurations.

Update Software Packages

Ensure that all software packages are up to date:

```
$ sudo apt update

$ sudo apt upgrade
```

Re-audit the System

- After implementing the hardening measures and addressing vulnerabilities, run another system audit to verify the improvements:

```
$ sudo lynis audit system
```

- Review the new audit results to ensure that the issues have been resolved and the system's security posture has improved.

Schedule Regular Audits

- Schedule regular audits to maintain system security. Create a cron job to run Lynis periodically:

```
$ sudo crontab -e
```

- Add the following line to run Lynis every week:

```
0 3 * * 1 /usr/bin/lynis audit system --cronjob
```

This cron job will run Lynis every Monday at 3 AM and email the results to the system administrator. Always keep AlphaProject safe and in compliance by using Lynis to conduct frequent security audits. Lynis can help you improve your system's security by revealing possible vulnerabilities and misconfigurations.

Periodical Security Updates and Patching

Security Updates/Patching Overview

Security updates and patches are released to fix vulnerabilities, bugs, and other security issues in software and operating systems. Regularly applying these updates helps protect your system against new threats and exploits. For AlphaProject, maintaining an updated system is crucial for preventing potential security breaches. This section will walkthrough you through using Lynis alongside built-in Linux commands and utilities to perform security updates and patches for AlphaProject.

Using Lynis for Security Updates and Patching

Lynis can help identify outdated packages and recommend security patches as part of its auditing process.

Running Lynis Audit

First, run a Lynis audit to check for outdated packages and necessary security updates:

```
$ sudo lynis audit system
```

Lynis will scan your system and list any outdated packages or security vulnerabilities that require attention.

Analyzing Lynis Output

Review the output from Lynis to identify packages that need updating. Look for sections in the report that highlight outdated software or recommended updates.

Following is the sample output:

```
System Information
```

```
------------------

[INFO] Outdated package(s) detected

 * Package 'libssl1.1' should be updated to version 1.1.1-1ubuntu2.1

 * Package 'apache2' should be updated to version 2.4.29-1ubuntu4.1


[INFO] Available security updates

 * 12 security updates available
```

Performing Security Updates using Linux Commands

Once you've identified the packages that need updating from the Lynis report, use the built-in Linux package management tools to apply these updates.

Updating the Package List

Start by updating the package list to ensure you have the latest information about available packages:

```
$ sudo apt update
```

This command retrieves the latest package lists from the configured repositories.

Upgrading Packages

- To upgrade all the installed packages to their latest versions, use the following command:

```
$ sudo apt upgrade
```

- This command installs the latest versions of all packages currently installed on your system.

Applying Security Updates Only

- If you want to apply only security updates, use the **unattended-upgrades** package.

Install the **unattended-upgrades** package if it is not already installed:

```
$ sudo apt install unattended-upgrades
```

- Edit the configuration file to enable automatic security updates:

```
$ sudo nano /etc/apt/apt.conf.d/50unattended-upgrades
```

- Uncomment or add the following lines to enable security updates:

```
Unattended-Upgrade::Allowed-Origins {
 "${distro_id}:${distro_codename}-security";
 "${distro_id}:${distro_codename}-updates";
};
```

- Enable the **unattended-upgrades** service:

```
$ sudo dpkg-reconfigure --priority=low unattended-
upgrades
```

- This service will now automatically apply security updates as they become available.

Manual Security Updates

- For systems where automatic updates are not configured, manually apply security updates:

```
$ sudo apt list --upgradable
$ sudo apt install [package-name]
```

- Replace **[package-name]** with the names of the packages identified by Lynis as needing updates.

Automating Security Updates with Cron

To ensure your system remains updated without manual intervention, schedule regular updates using cron jobs.

Edit the crontab file to add a new cron job:

```
$ sudo crontab -e
```

Add the following line to run the update and upgrade commands weekly:

```
0 2 * * 0 apt update && apt upgrade -y
```

This cron job will run every Sunday at 2 AM, updating the package lists and upgrading all packages automatically.

Sample Program: Implementing Security Updates and Patching for AlphaProject

We shall go through a practical example of performing security updates and patching for AlphaProject using Lynis and built-in Linux commands.

Run Lynis Audit

Run a Lynis audit to identify outdated packages and security vulnerabilities:

```
$ sudo lynis audit system
```

Review Lynis Report

Review the Lynis report to identify packages that need updating. Note the specific packages and any available security updates.

Update Package List

Update the package list to ensure the latest information about available packages:

```
$ sudo apt update
```

Upgrade outdated Packages

Upgrade all installed packages to their latest versions:

```
$ sudo apt upgrade -y
```

Apply Security Updates

If necessary, apply only the security updates using **unattended-upgrades** or manually:

```
$ sudo unattended-upgrades --dry-run --verbose

$ sudo unattended-upgrades
```

Or manually:

```
$ sudo apt install [package-name]
```

Automate Security Updates

Automate the process by configuring cron to run updates regularly:

```
$ sudo crontab -e
```

Add the following line to schedule weekly updates:

```
0 2 * * 0 apt update && apt upgrade -y
```

Verify Updates

After running updates, verify that all packages are up to date:

```
$ sudo apt list --upgradable
```

Ensure that no packages are listed as upgradable.

Integrating Security Updates with Monitoring

To ensure you are always aware of the update status, integrate security updates with system monitoring tools. For example, you can use Nagios to monitor the update status and alert you when updates are available.

Install Monitoring Agent

Install a monitoring agent that integrates with your chosen monitoring tool. For Nagios, you might use NRPE:

```
$ sudo apt install nagios-nrpe-server
```

Configure Monitoring Checks

Configure a check in Nagios to monitor the update status. For Nagios, add a check command to the NRPE configuration:

```
$ sudo nano /etc/nagios/nrpe.cfg
```

Add the following line:

```
command[check_updates]=/usr/lib/nagios/plugins/check_apt
```

Add Monitoring Check to Nagios

Add the new check to your Nagios configuration:

```
$ sudo nano /etc/nagios3/conf.d/localhost_nagios2.cfg
```

Add the following service definition:

```
define service {
 use generic-service
 host_name localhost
 service_description APT Updates
 check_command check_nrpe!check_updates
}
```

Restart Monitoring Service

Restart the Nagios service to apply the new configuration:

```
$ sudo systemctl restart nagios3
```

By following these steps, you can ensure that AlphaProject is regularly updated and patched. This practice helps maintain system security and minimizes the risk of vulnerabilities being exploited. Lynis provides valuable insights into which packages need updates, and built-in Linux commands and tools make it easy to apply these updates efficiently.

Introduction to Snort

Overview

Snort offers real-time traffic analysis and packet logging on IP networks; it is an open-source NIDS and IPS. It finds widespread use in keeping tabs on network traffic and identifying potentially malicious or policy-violating actions. Among Snort's many features are the ability to analyze protocols, search for and match content, and use a number of preprocessors. It uses a flexible rule-based language to describe traffic patterns.

How Snort Works?

Snort operates in several modes:

- Sniffer Mode: Reads network packets and displays them on the console.
- Packet Logger Mode: Logs packets to disk.
- Network Intrusion Detection Mode: Analyzes network traffic against user-defined rules and alerts the user when suspicious activity is detected.

Snort uses a rule-based language for defining patterns to match against packet data. Rules consist of headers and options, where headers specify which packets to inspect, and options define what to look for within those packets. When a packet matches a rule, Snort generates an alert or performs a predefined action.

Installing and Configuring Snort

We shall install and configure Snort on an Ubuntu system for AlphaProject.

Install Snort

Update the package list and install Snort:

```
$ sudo apt update

$ sudo apt install snort
```

During installation, you will be prompted to configure the network interface that Snort should listen to. Choose the appropriate interface (e.g., **eth0**).

Verify Installation

Check the Snort version to verify the installation:

```
$ snort -V
```

Following is the sample output:

```
,,_ -*> Snort! <*-

 o" )~ Version 2.9.15.0 GRE (Build 149)

 '''' By Martin Roesch & The Snort Team

 http://www.snort.org/contact#team

 Copyright (C) 2014-2020 Cisco and/or its affiliates. All
Rights Reserved.
```

Configure Snort

Snort's main configuration file is located at **/etc/snort/snort.conf**. Open this file in a text editor to configure the necessary settings:

```
$ sudo nano /etc/snort/snort.conf
```

Set Network Variables

In the configuration file, set the network variables for your environment. For AlphaProject, define the HOME_NET and EXTERNAL_NET variables:

```
var HOME_NET 192.168.1.0/24

var EXTERNAL_NET any
```

Configure Preprocessors

Snort preprocessors enhance its detection capabilities. Ensure the following preprocessors are enabled in the configuration file:

```
preprocessor stream5_global: track_tcp yes, track_udp yes
```

```
preprocessor stream5_tcp: policy linux, timeout 30,
min_ttl 10, max_tcp 8192, require_3whs 180, overlap_limit
10, small_segments 3 bytes 150

preprocessor stream5_udp: timeout 30

preprocessor stream5_icmp: timeout 30

preprocessor http_inspect: global iis_unicode_map
unicode.map 1252

preprocessor http_inspect_server: server default profile
all ports { 80 8080 }
```

Include Snort Rules

Snort rules are located in the **/etc/snort/rules/** directory. Ensure the rules are included in the configuration file:

```
include $RULE_PATH/local.rules

include $RULE_PATH/community.rules
```

Create Local Rules

Create a local rule file to define custom rules specific to AlphaProject:

```
$ sudo nano /etc/snort/rules/local.rules
```

Add a simple rule to detect ICMP ping requests:

```
alert icmp any any -> $HOME_NET any (msg:"ICMP Ping
detected"; sid:1000001; rev:1;)
```

Test Snort Configuration

Test the Snort configuration to ensure there are no syntax errors:

```
$ sudo snort -T -c /etc/snort/snort.conf
```

Run Snort in NIDS Mode

Start Snort in network intrusion detection mode:

```
$ sudo snort -A console -c /etc/snort/snort.conf -i eth0
```

Snort will start monitoring network traffic and display alerts on the console for any packets that match the defined rules.

Automate Snort

To run Snort as a daemon and ensure it starts on boot, create a systemd service file:

```
$ sudo nano /etc/systemd/system/snort.service
```

Add the following content to the service file:

```
[Unit]

Description=Snort NIDS Daemon

After=network.target


[Service]

ExecStart=/usr/sbin/snort -D -c /etc/snort/snort.conf -i
eth0

ExecReload=/bin/kill -HUP $MAINPID


[Install]

WantedBy=multi-user.target
```

Enable and start the Snort service:

```
$ sudo systemctl enable snort

$ sudo systemctl start snort
```

Verify the status of the Snort service:

```
$ sudo systemctl status snort
```

Following is the sample output:

```
snort.service - Snort NIDS Daemon

 Loaded: loaded (/etc/systemd/system/snort.service;
enabled; vendor preset: enabled)

 Active: active (running) since Mon 2024-05-27 10:00:00
UTC; 10min ago

 Main PID: 1234 (snort)

 Tasks: 1 (limit: 2332)

 CGroup: /system.slice/snort.service

  └─1234 /usr/sbin/snort -D -c /etc/snort/snort.conf -i
eth0
```

With this, now Snort is actively monitoring network traffic for AlphaProject and generating alerts based on the configured rules.

Monitoring System Logs for Security

Keeping an eye on system logs is an important part of keeping systems secure. Whether a login attempt succeeded or failed, any application errors, and any other noteworthy events are detailed in the system logs. Administrators can find security risks and fix them by methodically retrieving, analyzing, and reviewing these logs. In this section, we will go over the steps to take in order to manage system logs efficiently, and then show you how to use Snort to monitor and analyze these logs for security issues.

Defining Log Management Process

To effectively manage and monitor system logs, follow these steps:

1. Use a centralized logging system to collect logs from multiple sources, making it easier to analyze and correlate events.
2. Schedule automated tasks to pull logs regularly, ensuring timely availability for analysis.
3. Standardize log formats to facilitate easier analysis and correlation.
4. Use indexing tools to store logs efficiently, enabling quick searches and retrieval.
5. Use log analysis tools to identify patterns, anomalies, and potential security incidents.
6. Set up alerts for specific events or patterns that indicate potential security threats.
7. Periodically review logs and alerts to ensure continuous monitoring and improvement.

Centralizing Log Collection

Centralizing log collection simplifies log management and analysis. Tools like **rsyslog** and **Syslog-ng** can be used to collect and forward logs to a central server.

Install rsyslog

On Ubuntu, **rsyslog** is installed by default. If it's not installed, you can install it using:

```
$ sudo apt update

$ sudo apt install rsyslog
```

Configure rsyslog to Forward Logs

Edit the **rsyslog** configuration file to forward logs to a central server:

```
$ sudo nano /etc/rsyslog.conf
```

Add the following lines to forward logs to a central server (replace **logserver.gitforgits.com** with your log server's hostname or IP address):

```
*.* @logserver.gitforgits.com:514
```

Restart the **rsyslog** service to apply the changes:

```
$ sudo systemctl restart rsyslog
```

Automating Log Pulling

Automate the process of pulling logs using cron jobs or similar scheduling tools.

Create a Script to Pull Logs

Create a script to pull logs from the system and forward them to the central log server:

```
$ sudo nano /usr/local/bin/pull_logs.sh
```

Add the following content to the script:

```
#!/bin/bash


# Pull logs from /var/log

rsync -avz /var/log/
user@logserver.gitforgits.com:/path/to/central/logs/


# Additional commands to process logs can be added here
```

Make the script executable:

```
$ sudo chmod +x /usr/local/bin/pull_logs.sh
```

Schedule the Script

Schedule the script to run periodically using cron:

```
$ sudo crontab -e
```

Add the following line to run the script every hour:

```
0 * * * * /usr/local/bin/pull_logs.sh
```

Normalizing Logs

Standardize log formats to facilitate easier analysis and correlation. Tools like Logstash can help in normalizing logs.

Install Logstash

Install Logstash on the central log server:

```
$ sudo apt update

$ sudo apt install logstash
```

Configure Logstash

Create a Logstash configuration file to process and normalize logs:

```
$ sudo nano /etc/logstash/conf.d/logstash.conf
```

Add the following content to the configuration file:

```
input {

 file {

 path => "/path/to/central/logs/*.log"

 start_position => "beginning"

 }

}


filter {

 grok {
```

```
 match => { "message" => "%{COMMONAPACHELOG}" }
 }
}

output {
 elasticsearch {
 hosts => ["localhost:9200"]
 index => "logs-%{+YYYY.MM.dd}"
 }
 stdout { codec => rubydebug }
}
```

Start the Logstash service:

```
$ sudo systemctl start logstash
```

Indexing and Storing Logs

Use tools like Elasticsearch to index and store logs, enabling quick searches and retrieval.

Install Elasticsearch

Install Elasticsearch on the central log server:

```
$ sudo apt update
$ sudo apt install elasticsearch
```

Configure Elasticsearch

Edit the Elasticsearch configuration file:

```
$ sudo nano /etc/elasticsearch/elasticsearch.yml
```

Configure the following settings:

```
network.host: localhost

http.port: 9200
```

Start the Elasticsearch service:

```
$ sudo systemctl start elasticsearch
```

Analyzing Logs

Use Kibana to visualize and analyze logs stored in Elasticsearch.

Install Kibana

Install Kibana on the central log server:

```
$ sudo apt update

$ sudo apt install kibana
```

Configure Kibana

Edit the Kibana configuration file:

```
$ sudo nano /etc/kibana/kibana.yml
```

Configure the following settings:

```
server.host: "localhost"

elasticsearch.hosts: ["http://localhost:9200"]
```

Start the Kibana service:

```
$ sudo systemctl start kibana
```

Access Kibana

Access Kibana via a web browser at **http://localhost:5601**. Use Kibana to create visualizations and dashboards for log analysis.

Setting up Alerts

Use Kibana's alerting features to set up alerts for specific events or patterns.

In Kibana, go to the "Alerting" section and create new alerts based on the logs stored in Elasticsearch. Define the conditions and actions for each alert. And, then monitor the alerts and take appropriate actions when alerts are triggered.

Using Snort for Log Monitoring and Security Assessment

Now, we shall integrate Snort to perform security monitoring and assessment of system logs.

Configure Snort to Log Alerts

Edit the Snort configuration file to enable logging of alerts:

```
$ sudo nano /etc/snort/snort.conf
```

Ensure the following lines are configured:

```
output unified2: filename snort.u2, limit 128
```

Create Snort Rules

Create custom Snort rules to detect specific patterns or anomalies in network traffic. Add these rules to the **local.rules** file:

```
$ sudo nano /etc/snort/rules/local.rules
```

Add a rule to detect SSH brute force attempts:

```
alert tcp any any -> $HOME_NET 22 (msg:"SSH Brute Force
Attempt"; flow:to_server,established;
detection_filter:track by_src, count 5, seconds 120;
sid:1000002; rev:1;)
```

Start Snort

Start Snort to begin monitoring and logging alerts:

```
$ sudo snort -A console -c /etc/snort/snort.conf -i eth0
```

Snort will now monitor network traffic and log alerts based on the defined rules.

Pull Snort Logs

Use the previously created script to pull Snort logs to the central log server. Update the script to include Snort logs:

```
$ sudo nano /usr/local/bin/pull_logs.sh
```

Add the following lines:

```
# Pull Snort logs

rsync -avz /var/log/snort/
user@logserver.gitforgits.com:/path/to/central/snort/logs
/
```

Analyze Snort Logs with Kibana

Configure Logstash to process Snort logs. Update the Logstash configuration file:

```
$ sudo nano /etc/logstash/conf.d/logstash.conf
```

Add the following input configuration for Snort logs:

```
input {
```

```
 file {
 path => "/path/to/central/snort/logs/snort.u2"
 codec => "json"
 start_position => "beginning"
 }
}
```

Restart Logstash to apply the changes:

```
$ sudo systemctl restart logstash
```

Then, create visualizations and dashboards for Snort logs. Use the data to identify potential security incidents and patterns.

By now, you will be able to use Snort or another log management tool to effectively monitor system logs for security. In order to identify and react quickly to possible security threats, this method guarantees thorough monitoring and evaluation of system logs.

Intrusion Detection Systems

Introduction to Intrusion Detection and Prevention

Intrusion Detection Systems, also known as IDS, are essential technologies for monitoring network traffic and identifying malicious activities or unauthorized access. IDS keep an eye on all of the data flowing through a network, looking for any signs of potential danger. A further step is taken by Intrusion Prevention Systems (IPS), which actively block or prevent threats that are detected. For network environments like AlphaProject, Snort's dual functionality as an IDS and an IPS provides strong protection.

In this section we will show you how to use Snort to keep your network secure by identifying and blocking potential threats.

Configuring Snort for Intrusion Detection

We have already installed and configured Snort in the previous sections. We shall now configure Snort to detect specific types of intrusions.

Define Detection Rules

Snort uses rules to detect patterns of malicious activity. These rules specify the conditions under which an alert should be generated. Rules consist of a header and options, where the header defines the rule's action, protocol, source and destination IPs, and ports, and the options specify the content to match.

Following is the sample rule to detect SSH brute force attacks:

```
alert tcp any any -> $HOME_NET 22 (msg:"SSH Brute Force
Attempt"; flow:to_server,established;
detection_filter:track by_src, count 5, seconds 120;
sid:1000002; rev:1;)
```

In the above snippet,

- **alert** specifies that Snort should generate an alert.
- **tcp** indicates the rule applies to TCP packets.
- **any any -> $HOME_NET 22** matches any source IP and port to destination IPs in **$HOME_NET** on port 22 (SSH).
- **msg** provides a message for the alert; **detection_filter** limits alerts to repeated attempts; **sid** is the rule identifier; **rev** is the rule revision.

Add Rules to Local Rules File

Edit the **local.rules** file to add custom detection rules:

```
$ sudo nano /etc/snort/rules/local.rules
```

Add the SSH brute force detection rule:

```
alert tcp any any -> $HOME_NET 22 (msg:"SSH Brute Force
Attempt"; flow:to_server,established;
detection_filter:track by_src, count 5, seconds 120;
sid:1000002; rev:1;)
```

Test Snort Configuration

Test the Snort configuration to ensure there are no syntax errors:

```
$ sudo snort -T -c /etc/snort/snort.conf
```

Start Snort in Detection Mode

Start Snort in network intrusion detection mode:

```
$ sudo snort -A console -c /etc/snort/snort.conf -i eth0
```

Snort will now monitor network traffic and generate alerts for any SSH brute force attempts.

Using Snort for Intrusion Prevention

To configure Snort as an Intrusion Prevention System (IPS), we will use the inline mode. This mode allows Snort to actively drop or modify packets that match predefined rules.

Install Necessary Packages

Ensure you have the **`libnetfilter-queue`** library installed:

```
$ sudo apt install libnetfilter-queue-dev
```

Modify Snort Configuration for Inline Mode

Edit the Snort configuration file to enable inline mode:

```
$ sudo nano /etc/snort/snort.conf
```

Ensure the following lines are included:

```
config policy_mode:inline
```

Define Prevention Rules

Add rules to drop packets that match specific patterns. For example, to drop SSH brute force attempts:

```
drop tcp any any -> $HOME_NET 22 (msg:"SSH Brute Force
Attempt"; flow:to_server,established;
detection_filter:track by_src, count 5, seconds 120;
sid:1000003; rev:1;)
```

Add this rule to the **local.rules** file:

```
$ sudo nano /etc/snort/rules/local.rules
```

Add the prevention rule:

```
drop tcp any any -> $HOME_NET 22 (msg:"SSH Brute Force
Attempt"; flow:to_server,established;
detection_filter:track by_src, count 5, seconds 120;
sid:1000003; rev:1;)
```

Configure iptables for Inline Mode

Configure **iptables** to pass packets to Snort using the **NFQUEUE** target:

```
$ sudo iptables -I INPUT -p tcp --dport 22 -j NFQUEUE --
queue-num 0
```

This command inserts a rule to send incoming TCP packets on port 22 (SSH) to NFQUEUE 0.

Start Snort in Inline Mode

Start Snort in inline mode to actively drop malicious packets:

```
$ sudo snort -Q --daq nfq --daq-mode inline -c
/etc/snort/snort.conf -i eth0
```

Snort will now operate in inline mode, monitoring traffic and dropping packets that match the defined prevention rules.

Sample Program: Utilizing Snort as an IDS and IPS

We shall perform a practical example using Snort to detect and prevent an SSH brute force attack on AlphaProject.

Define Detection and Prevention Rules

Edit the **`local.rules`** file to add both detection and prevention rules for SSH brute force attempts:

```
$ sudo nano /etc/snort/rules/local.rules
```

Add the following rules:

```
alert tcp any any -> $HOME_NET 22 (msg:"SSH Brute Force
Attempt"; flow:to_server,established;
detection_filter:track by_src, count 5, seconds 120;
sid:1000002; rev:1;)

drop tcp any any -> $HOME_NET 22 (msg:"SSH Brute Force
Attempt"; flow:to_server,established;
detection_filter:track by_src, count 5, seconds 120;
sid:1000003; rev:1;)
```

Configure iptables for Inline Mode

Add an iptables rule to forward SSH traffic to Snort's NFQUEUE:

```
$ sudo iptables -I INPUT -p tcp --dport 22 -j NFQUEUE --
queue-num 0
```

Start Snort in Inline Mode

Start Snort in inline mode:

```
$ sudo snort -Q --daq nfq --daq-mode inline -c
/etc/snort/snort.conf -i eth0
```

Simulate an SSH Brute Force Attack

Use a tool like Hydra to simulate an SSH brute force attack on AlphaProject:

```
$ hydra -l root -P /path/to/password/list.txt
ssh://192.168.1.100
```

Monitor Snort Alerts

Monitor the Snort console for alerts indicating SSH brute force attempts. Snort should generate alerts for detection and drop packets based on prevention rules.

Following is the desired output of the Alert:

```
[**] [1:1000002:1] SSH Brute Force Attempt [**]

[Classification: Attempted Administrator Privilege Gain]
[Priority: 1]

03/15-13:15:22.123456 192.168.1.105:56345 ->
192.168.1.100:22

TCP TTL:64 TOS:0x0 ID:12345 IpLen:20 DgmLen:60 DF

***AP*** Seq: 0x1A2B3C4D Ack: 0x5E6F7A8B Win: 0x2000
TcpLen: 40

TCP Options (3) => NOP NOP TS: 1234567890 1234567890


[**] [1:1000003:1] SSH Brute Force Attempt [**]

[Classification: Attempted Administrator Privilege Gain]
[Priority: 1]

03/15-13:15:22.123456 192.168.1.105:56345 ->
192.168.1.100:22

TCP TTL:64 TOS:0x0 ID:12345 IpLen:20 DgmLen:60 DF

***AP*** Seq: 0x1A2B3C4D Ack: 0x5E6F7A8B Win: 0x2000
TcpLen: 40
```

```
TCP Options (3) => NOP NOP TS: 1234567890 1234567890
```

By following these steps, you can effectively use Snort to detect and prevent intrusions on your network. This setup enhances the security posture of AlphaProject by providing real-time detection and prevention of potential threats.

Securing SSH Access

Secure Shell (SSH) is a protocol used for secure remote login and other secure network services over an insecure network. While SSH provides a secure channel, it can still be a target for attacks such as brute force attempts, man-in-the-middle attacks, and unauthorized access. Implementing additional security measures can significantly reduce these risks.

Following are the techniques to secure SSH access:

- Disabling Root Login
- Using Key-Based Authentication
- Changing the Default SSH Port
- Limiting User Access
- Enforcing Strong Password Policies
- Using Two-Factor Authentication (2FA)
- Configuring SSH with Fail2Ban

Disabling Root Login

Disabling root login prevents attackers from directly accessing the root account, which has the highest privileges.

Open the SSH configuration file:

```
$ sudo nano /etc/ssh/sshd_config
```

Find the following line and set it to **no**:

```
PermitRootLogin no
```

Restart the SSH service to apply the changes:

```
$ sudo systemctl restart sshd
```

Using Key-Based Authentication

Key-based authentication provides a more secure method of logging into SSH than password authentication.

Generate a key pair on the client machine:

```
$ ssh-keygen -t rsa -b 4096
```

Copy the public key to the server using **ssh-copy-id**:

```
$ ssh-copy-id user@server_ip
```

Edit the SSH configuration file to disable password authentication:

```
$ sudo nano /etc/ssh/sshd_config
```

Set the following line to **no**:

```
PasswordAuthentication no
```

Restart the SSH service:

```
$ sudo systemctl restart sshd
```

Changing Default SSH Port

Changing the default SSH port (22) can reduce the risk of automated attacks targeting the default port.

Open the SSH configuration file:

```
$ sudo nano /etc/ssh/sshd_config
```

Find the following line and change the port number:

```
Port 2222
```

Update the firewall rules to allow the new SSH port:

```
$ sudo ufw allow 2222/tcp
```

Restart the SSH service:

```
$ sudo systemctl restart sshd
```

Limiting User Access

Restricting SSH access to specific users or groups can further secure your system.

Open the SSH configuration file:

```
$ sudo nano /etc/ssh/sshd_config
```

Add the following lines to restrict access:

```
AllowUsers user1 user2

AllowGroups sshusers
```

Restart the SSH service:

```
$ sudo systemctl restart sshd
```

Enforcing Strong Password Policies

Ensure users set strong passwords to enhance security. At first, install the **libpam-pwquality** module:

```
$ sudo apt install libpam-pwquality
```

Edit the PAM configuration for passwords:

```
$ sudo nano /etc/pam.d/common-password
```

Add the following line to enforce strong passwords:

```
password requisite pam_pwquality.so retry=3 minlen=12
difok=3
```

Using Two-Factor Authentication (2FA)

Adding an extra layer of security with two-factor authentication can prevent unauthorized access even if passwords are compromised.

Install the Google Authenticator PAM module:

```
$ sudo apt install libpam-google-authenticator
```

Run the following command for each user to set up 2FA:

```
$ google-authenticator
```

Address the prompts to configure 2FA for the user. Edit the SSH PAM configuration file:

```
$ sudo nano /etc/pam.d/sshd
```

Add the following line:

```
auth required pam_google_authenticator.so
```

Edit the SSH configuration file:

```
$ sudo nano /etc/ssh/sshd_config
```

Ensure the following lines are set:

```
ChallengeResponseAuthentication yes
```

Restart the SSH service:

```
$ sudo systemctl restart sshd
```

Configuring SSH with Fail2Ban

Fail2Ban helps protect against brute force attacks by banning IP addresses that show malicious signs.

Install Fail2Ban:

```
$ sudo apt install fail2ban
```

Create a local configuration file:

```
$ sudo nano /etc/fail2ban/jail.local
```

Add the following configuration for SSH:

```
[sshd]

enabled = true

port = 2222

filter = sshd

logpath = /var/log/auth.log

maxretry = 3
```

Restart the Fail2Ban service:

```
$ sudo systemctl restart fail2ban
```

Check the status of Fail2Ban to ensure it is working correctly:

```
$ sudo fail2ban-client status sshd
```

Following is the sample output:

```
Status for the jail: sshd

|- Filter
```

```
| |- Currently failed: 1
| |- Total failed: 5
| `- File list: /var/log/auth.log
`- Actions
  |- Currently banned: 1
  |- Total banned: 1
  `- Banned IP list: 192.168.1.105
```

By implementing these techniques, you can significantly enhance the security of SSH access for AlphaProject. These measures help protect against unauthorized access, brute force attacks, and other potential security threats.

Configuring VPNs for Secure Connections

Introduction to VPNs

Virtual Private Networks (VPNs) create a secure connection between your local network and remote networks over the internet. This is particularly useful for AlphaProject, where secure remote access is necessary. VPNs use encryption to secure data transmitted over public networks, ensuring that only authorized users can access the network. OpenVPN is a popular open-source VPN solution that supports both client-server and peer-to-peer configurations. In this section, we will configure an OpenVPN server and client to establish a secure connection.

Setting up OpenVPN Server

To set up an OpenVPN server on your Ubuntu system, follow these steps:

Install OpenVPN and Easy-RSA

First, install OpenVPN and Easy-RSA, a toolkit for managing SSL/TLS certificates:

```
$ sudo apt update
$ sudo apt install openvpn easy-rsa
```

Configure Easy-RSA

Copy the Easy-RSA scripts to a new directory and navigate to it:

```
$ make-cadir ~/openvpn-ca

$ cd ~/openvpn-ca
```

Edit the **vars** file to set your CA variables:

```
$ nano vars
```

Set the following values according to your requirements:

```
set_var EASYRSA_REQ_COUNTRY "US"

set_var EASYRSA_REQ_PROVINCE "California"

set_var EASYRSA_REQ_CITY "San Francisco"

set_var EASYRSA_REQ_ORG "AlphaProject"

set_var EASYRSA_REQ_EMAIL "admin@alphaproject.com"

set_var EASYRSA_REQ_OU "AlphaProject VPN"
```

Build the CA

Source the **vars** file and clean up any existing keys:

```
$ source vars

$ ./clean-all
```

Build the Certificate Authority (CA):

```
$ ./easyrsa build-ca
```

Follow the prompts to set the CA password and generate the CA certificate.

Generate Server Certificate and Key

```
$ ./easyrsa gen-req server nopass

$ ./easyrsa sign-req server server
```

Generate Diffie-Hellman Parameters

```
$ ./easyrsa gen-dh
```

Generate Client Certificate and Key

```
$ ./easyrsa gen-req client1 nopass

$ ./easyrsa sign-req client client1
```

Configure OpenVPN

Create a directory to store the server configuration files:

```
$ sudo mkdir -p /etc/openvpn/server
```

Copy the generated files to the OpenVPN directory:

```
$ sudo cp pki/ca.crt pki/private/server.key
pki/issued/server.crt pki/dh.pem /etc/openvpn/server
```

Create the OpenVPN server configuration file:

```
$ sudo nano /etc/openvpn/server/server.conf
```

Add the following configuration:

```
port 1194

proto udp
```

```
dev tun

ca ca.crt

cert server.crt

key server.key

dh dh.pem

server 10.8.0.0 255.255.255.0

ifconfig-pool-persist ipp.txt

push "redirect-gateway def1 bypass-dhcp"

push "dhcp-option DNS 8.8.8.8"

push "dhcp-option DNS 8.8.4.4"

keepalive 10 120

cipher AES-256-CBC

user nobody

group nogroup

persist-key

persist-tun

status openvpn-status.log

verb 3
```

Enable IP Forwarding

Enable IP forwarding to allow traffic to flow between the VPN and the internet:

```
$ sudo nano /etc/sysctl.conf
```

Uncomment the following line:

```
net.ipv4.ip_forward=1
```

Apply the changes:

```
$ sudo sysctl -p
```

Configure UFW

Allow OpenVPN traffic through the firewall and configure NAT:

```
$ sudo ufw allow 1194/udp

$ sudo nano /etc/ufw/before.rules
```

Add the following rules at the top of the file:

```
*nat

:POSTROUTING ACCEPT [0:0]

-A POSTROUTING -s 10.8.0.0/8 -o eth0 -j MASQUERADE

COMMIT
```

Enable UFW forwarding:

```
$ sudo nano /etc/default/ufw
```

Set the following:

```
DEFAULT_FORWARD_POLICY="ACCEPT"
```

Restart UFW:

```
$ sudo ufw disable
```

```
$ sudo ufw enable
```

Start and Enable OpenVPN Service

```
$ sudo systemctl start openvpn@server

$ sudo systemctl enable openvpn@server
```

Configuring OpenVPN Client

Install OpenVPN

```
$ sudo apt update

$ sudo apt install openvpn
```

Create Client Configuration File

Create a client configuration file on the client machine:

```
$ nano client.ovpn
```

Add the following configuration:

```
client

dev tun

proto udp

remote your_server_ip 1194

resolv-retry infinite

nobind

user nobody

group nogroup
```

```
persist-key

persist-tun

ca ca.crt

cert client1.crt

key client1.key

remote-cert-tls server

cipher AES-256-CBC

verb 3
```

Transfer Client Files

Transfer the **ca.crt**, **client1.crt**, and **client1.key** files from the server to the client:

```
$ scp user@server_ip:/path/to/ca.crt /path/to/client/

$ scp user@server_ip:/path/to/client1.crt
/path/to/client/

$ scp user@server_ip:/path/to/client1.key
/path/to/client/
```

Connect to the VPN

On the client machine, start the OpenVPN client using the configuration file:

```
$ sudo openvpn --config client.ovpn
```

Now the client can attach to the OpenVPN server and set up a private VPN connection. This configuration encrypts data sent over the network and grants secure access to the AlphaProject environment, ensuring that remote connections are secure.

Managing Certificates and Encryption

Introduction to Certificates and Encryption

Authenticating the identities of users, devices, and services, as well as ensuring the confidentiality of communications through encryption, are all accomplished through the utilization of public key infrastructure (PKI) by certificates. A reputable certificate authority (CA) issues certificates, which include the owner's identity and a public key. Data transmitted over a network can be certain that it will remain private and safe from prying eyes thanks to encryption.

In this section, we will learn how to create and encrypt certificates, and then we will show you how to use them in AlphaProject.

Generating Certificates

To generate and manage certificates for AlphaProject, we will use OpenSSL, a robust toolkit for SSL/TLS encryption.

Install OpenSSL

Ensure OpenSSL is installed on your system:

```
$ sudo apt update

$ sudo apt install openssl
```

Generate a Private Key

The first step in creating a certificate is to generate a private key. This key will be used to create the certificate signing request (CSR) and later to decrypt the data encrypted by the public key.

```
$ openssl genpkey -algorithm RSA -out private.key -aes256
```

You will be prompted to enter a passphrase to protect the private key.

Generate a Certificate Signing Request (CSR)

Next, generate a CSR, which will be sent to the CA to obtain a signed certificate:

```
$ openssl req -new -key private.key -out server.csr
```

You will be prompted to enter information about your organization and the server:

```
Country Name (2 letter code) [AU]:US
```

```
State or Province Name (full name) [Some-
State]:California

Locality Name (eg, city) []:San Francisco

Organization Name (eg, company) [Internet Widgits Pty
Ltd]:AlphaProject

Organizational Unit Name (eg, section) []:IT Department

Common Name (e.g. server FQDN or YOUR name)
[]:alphaproject.com

Email Address []:admin@alphaproject.com
```

Generate a Self-Signed Certificate

For internal use or testing, you can generate a self-signed certificate. This type of certificate is signed with your own private key rather than by a CA:

```
$ openssl req -x509 -days 365 -key private.key -in
server.csr -out server.crt
```

This command creates a certificate valid for 365 days.

Encrypting Certificates

Encrypting certificates ensures they are securely stored and transmitted. OpenSSL uses the private key to encrypt data, which can only be decrypted by the corresponding public key.

Encrypt the Private Key

The private key is already encrypted if you used the **-aes256** option when generating it. To verify, you can use:

```
$ openssl rsa -in private.key -check
```

Encrypt Communication Using the Certificate

To use the generated certificates in a secure communication setup, such as an HTTPS server or

VPN, you need to configure the server to use these certificates.

Using Certificates in AlphaProject

Let us configure an HTTPS server (Apache) to use the generated certificates for secure communication in AlphaProject.

Ensure Apache is installed:

```
$ sudo apt update

$ sudo apt install apache2
```

Enable the SSL module and the default SSL site:

```
$ sudo a2enmod ssl

$ sudo a2ensite default-ssl

$ sudo systemctl reload apache2
```

Copy the generated certificates to the appropriate directory:

```
$ sudo cp server.crt /etc/ssl/certs/

$ sudo cp private.key /etc/ssl/private/
```

Edit the SSL configuration file:

```
$ sudo nano /etc/apache2/sites-available/default-ssl.conf
```

Update the following lines to point to your certificate and private key files:

```
SSLCertificateFile /etc/ssl/certs/server.crt

SSLCertificateKeyFile /etc/ssl/private/private.key
```

Restart Apache to apply the changes:

```
$ sudo systemctl restart apache2
```

Apache is now configured to use the SSL certificate and private key for HTTPS connections.

Sample Program: Managing Certificates and Implementing Encryption

We shall now implement the full procedure for AlphaProject, starting with creating the certificates and ending with setting up an Apache server for HTTPS.

Generate a private key:

```
$ openssl genpkey -algorithm RSA -out alphaproject.key -
aes256
```

Generate a CSR:

```
$ openssl req -new -key alphaproject.key -out
alphaproject.csr
```

Fill in the organization details:

```
Country Name (2 letter code) [AU]:US

State or Province Name (full name) [Some-
State]:California

Locality Name (eg, city) []:San Francisco

Organization Name (eg, company) [Internet Widgits Pty
Ltd]:AlphaProject

Organizational Unit Name (eg, section) []:IT Department

Common Name (e.g. server FQDN or YOUR name)
[]:alphaproject.com

Email Address []:admin@alphaproject.com
```

Generate the self-signed certificate:

```
$ openssl req -x509 -days 365 -key alphaproject.key -in
alphaproject.csr -out alphaproject.crt
```

Copy the certificates to the appropriate directories:

```
$ sudo cp alphaproject.crt /etc/ssl/certs/

$ sudo cp alphaproject.key /etc/ssl/private/
```

Edit the Apache SSL configuration file:

```
$ sudo nano /etc/apache2/sites-available/default-ssl.conf
```

Update the configuration to use the new certificates:

```
SSLCertificateFile /etc/ssl/certs/alphaproject.crt

SSLCertificateKeyFile /etc/ssl/private/alphaproject.key
```

Restart the Apache server to apply the changes:

```
$ sudo systemctl restart apache2
```

With the self-signed certificate and encrypted private key, your Apache server for AlphaProject is now set up to use SSL/TLS, guaranteeing secure HTTPS connections. This configuration prevents eavesdropping and tampering with data transmitted between clients and the server.

Summary

This chapter taught you how to better secure your Linux systems with the necessary tools and techniques. In the first part of the chapter, we looked at two powerful tools for managing firewall rules, iptables and firewalld. In it, the configuration steps for these tools to manage network traffic and prevent unauthorized access were laid out in detail. In the section on implementing AppArmor, we covered how to set up and enforce AppArmor policies, and we also introduced the idea of using security profiles to limit the capabilities of applications.

Following this, the chapter delves further into the topic of conducting security audits using Lynis.

We then covered the basics of installing and configuring Lynis, as well as how to run security audits and understand the resultant information to fix vulnerabilities. We also went over how to apply patches and security updates on a regular basis, using Lynis and the Linux command line, to keep the system safe and secure.

While introducing Snort, we covered its features and how it can help with intrusion detection and prevention. You will find detailed instructions on how to set up Snort to monitor your network traffic and identify possible intrusions. The section on monitoring system logs for security emphasized the importance of centralized log collection and automated log pulling, showcasing how to use Snort for security monitoring and assessment.

Different methods for securing SSH access were detailed, such as enabling key-based authentication, changing the default SSH port, enabling two-factor authentication, and disabling root login. In order to set up a secure communication channel, we covered how to configure VPNs for secure connections, specifically going over the steps to set up an OpenVPN server and client. Finally, the chapter demonstrated how to generate and encrypt certificates using OpenSSL and configure them for secure communication in AlphaProject, covering the process of managing certificates and encryption.

CHAPTER 4: DATABASE MANAGEMENT

Introduction

The important aspects of database management in a Linux setting are covered in this chapter. Beginning with a general introduction to Linux databases, this chapter equips you with the background information you need to manage databases effectively. Next, you will find out how to set up PostgreSQL, a famous and powerful open-source relational database system that runs on Linux.

Next, you will find some pointers on how to build databases for Linux applications, with an emphasis on how to organize and structure data in a way that makes it efficient and scalable. It addresses database migrations, an essential competency for updating schemas of databases while minimizing the impact on live data and applications. Important for data security and catastrophe recovery, you will learn about backup and restore processes.

Additionally, the chapter explores the topic of database performance monitoring with Nagios, a popular tool for this purpose. Protecting sensitive data from unauthorized access is of utmost importance in database management. You will discover techniques to secure your database systems. Lastly, the chapter delves into the topic of automating database operations, which helps you to simplify repetitive tasks while ensuring consistent performance and reliability.

Database Working in Linux

Databases Compatible with Linux

Databases are crucial for managing and storing data efficiently, and Linux provides a robust environment for various database systems.Several databases are compatible with Linux, each catering to different needs and use cases:

1. PostgreSQL: A powerful, open-source object-relational database system known for its robustness and support for advanced data types and performance optimization.
2. MySQL/MariaDB: Popular open-source relational database management systems widely used in web applications. MariaDB is a fork of MySQL with additional features and improved performance.
3. SQLite: A lightweight, file-based database often used in embedded systems and small-scale applications.
4. MongoDB: A NoSQL database known for its flexibility in handling unstructured data, scalability, and ease of use.
5. Redis: An in-memory key-value store used for caching, session management, and real-time analytics.
6. Oracle Database: A robust, enterprise-level relational database management system known for its advanced features and scalability.
7. Microsoft SQL Server: Available on Linux since 2017, it offers a comprehensive relational

database solution with high availability and security features.

How Databases Perform in Linux Systems?

Databases on Linux perform efficiently due to the stability, performance, and flexibility that the Linux operating system offers. Given below is a deeper look at how databases operate in Linux environments and how they compare to Windows:

Stability and Performance

Linux is known for its stability and performance, making it a preferred choice for running database systems. The absence of unnecessary background processes and the efficient handling of system resources in Linux contribute to better database performance.

- Linux: Databases on Linux benefit from lower system overhead and better resource management. Linux's lightweight nature and efficient I/O handling lead to faster query processing and data retrieval.
- Windows: While Windows has improved significantly in terms of performance, it generally consumes more system resources compared to Linux. The graphical user interface and additional services can impact overall database performance.

Resource Management

Linux provides advanced resource management tools and features such as cgroups and namespaces, allowing precise control over system resources allocated to databases.

- Linux: Administrators can fine-tune system resources using tools like **htop**, **top**, and **vmstat**. This granular control helps in optimizing database performance by ensuring that critical processes receive adequate resources.
- Windows: Windows offers resource management tools like Task Manager and Resource Monitor, but they may not provide the same level of granularity and control as their Linux counterparts.

File System and I/O Performance

Linux supports various file systems like ext4, XFS, and Btrfs, which are optimized for different use cases and performance requirements. The choice of file system can significantly impact database performance.

- Linux: File systems like ext4 and XFS offer high performance and reliability, making them ideal for database operations. The asynchronous I/O capabilities in Linux further enhance database performance by allowing non-blocking operations.
- Windows: Windows primarily uses NTFS, which is robust but may not offer the same level of performance optimization for databases as Linux file systems.

Security and Access Control

Security is a critical aspect of database management, and Linux provides robust security features to protect databases from unauthorized access and vulnerabilities.

- Linux: Linux offers advanced security mechanisms such as SELinux, AppArmor, and iptables, providing fine-grained control over access permissions and network security. These features help in securing database environments effectively.
- Windows: Windows has strong security features like BitLocker and Windows Firewall, but the security model in Linux is often considered more flexible and customizable.

Networking and Connectivity

Databases often need to interact with other systems over the network, and Linux provides efficient networking capabilities to facilitate this.

- Linux: The networking stack in Linux is highly efficient, supporting various network configurations and protocols. Tools like **netstat**, **ss**, and **iptables** help in monitoring and securing network connections.
- Windows: Windows also supports robust networking features, but administrators might find the networking tools in Linux more versatile and powerful.

Customizability and Flexibility

One of the strengths of Linux is its customizability, allowing administrators to tailor the operating system to specific database requirements.

- Linux: Linux offers a high degree of customization, from kernel parameters to user-space utilities. This flexibility enables administrators to optimize the system for specific database workloads.
- Windows: While Windows allows customization, it is generally less flexible than Linux. The Windows environment is more standardized, which can be a limitation for advanced database tuning.

By understanding how databases work in Linux and comparing them to Windows, administrators can make informed decisions to optimize their database environments.

Installing and Configuring PostgreSQL

PostgreSQL is a powerful, open-source object-relational database system that is highly suitable for various applications, including AlphaProject. Now, we will demonstrate how to install, configure, and integrate PostgreSQL into our Linux environment or for our AlphaProject.

Installing PostgreSQL

Before installing PostgreSQL, ensure your package list is up to date:

```
$ sudo apt update
```

Install PostgreSQL and the contrib package, which provides additional tools and features:

```
$ sudo apt install postgresql postgresql-contrib
```

Check the status of the PostgreSQL service to ensure it is running:

```
$ sudo systemctl status postgresql
```

You should see output indicating that the PostgreSQL service is active and running.

Configuring PostgreSQL

Switch to the PostgreSQL user and access the PostgreSQL command line interface (psql):

```
$ sudo -i -u postgres

$ psql
```

You will enter the PostgreSQL command line interface, where you can manage your databases.

Create a new database for AlphaProject:

```
CREATE DATABASE alphaproject_db;
```

Create a new user with a password:

```
CREATE USER alphaproject_user WITH PASSWORD
'yourpassword';
```

Grant all privileges on the AlphaProject database to the new user:

```
GRANT ALL PRIVILEGES ON DATABASE alphaproject_db TO
alphaproject_user;
```

Exit the PostgreSQL command line interface:

```
\q
```

Edit the PostgreSQL authentication configuration file to allow password authentication. Open the **pg_hba.conf** file:

```
$ sudo nano /etc/postgresql/12/main/pg_hba.conf
```

Locate the lines that look like this:

```
# "local" is for Unix domain socket connections only

local all all peer

# IPv4 local connections:

host all all 127.0.0.1/32 md5

# IPv6 local connections:

host all all ::1/128 md5
```

Ensure that the method for local and remote connections is set to **md5** for password authentication. Save and close the file.

Restart PostgreSQL to apply the changes:

```
$ sudo systemctl restart postgresql
```

Integrating PostgreSQL with AlphaProject

Ensure that your development environment includes the necessary PostgreSQL client libraries. For example, if you are using Python, you can install the **psycopg2** library:

```
$ sudo apt install python3-psycopg2
```

For Node.js, you might install the **pg** package:

```
$ npm install pg
```

Configure your application to connect to the PostgreSQL database. For example, in a Python application using **psycopg2**:

```
import psycopg2


conn = psycopg2.connect(
 dbname="alphaproject_db",
 user="alphaproject_user",
 password="yourpassword",
 host="localhost"
)


cur = conn.cursor()
cur.execute("SELECT version();")
db_version = cur.fetchone()
print(db_version)
cur.close()
conn.close()
```

For a Node.js application using the **pg** package:

```
const { Client } = require('pg');
```

```
const client = new Client({
 user: 'alphaproject_user',
 host: 'localhost',
 database: 'alphaproject_db',
 password: 'yourpassword',
 port: 5432,
});

client.connect();

client.query('SELECT version()', (err, res) => {
 if (err) {
 console.error(err);
 } else {
 console.log(res.rows[0]);
 }
 client.end();
});
```

Ensure that your application's configuration file includes the correct database connection settings. For a Django application, update the **settings.py** file:

```
DATABASES = {
```

```
 'default': {
 'ENGINE': 'django.db.backends.postgresql',
 'NAME': 'alphaproject_db',
 'USER': 'alphaproject_user',
 'PASSWORD': 'yourpassword',
 'HOST': 'localhost',
 'PORT': '5432',
 }
}
```

For a Node.js application using environment variables:

```
const { Client } = require('pg');

const client = new Client({
 user: process.env.PGUSER,
 host: process.env.PGHOST,
 database: process.env.PGDATABASE,
 password: process.env.PGPASSWORD,
 port: process.env.PGPORT,
});

client.connect();
```

Create scripts to initialize your database with necessary tables and data for AlphaProject. For example, in SQL:

```
CREATE TABLE users (

 id SERIAL PRIMARY KEY,

 username VARCHAR(50) UNIQUE NOT NULL,

 password VARCHAR(50) NOT NULL,

 email VARCHAR(100) NOT NULL

);


INSERT INTO users (username, password, email) VALUES
('admin', 'adminpass', 'admin@alphaproject.com');
```

Save the script and execute it using the **psql** command-line tool:

```
$ psql -U alphaproject_user -d alphaproject_db -f
init_db.sql
```

With this command, the SQL script will be executed, and the database's initial schema and data will be set up. After you've followed these steps, PostgreSQL will be installed, configured, and integrated into the AlphaProject Linux environment.

Database Design for Linux Programs

Introduction to Database Design

Database design involves defining the tables, columns, relationships, and constraints that organize and store the data. A well-designed schema improves performance, ensures data consistency, and makes maintenance easier. For AlphaProject, we will create a relational database schema using PostgreSQL.

Step-by-Step Database Schema Design

Before designing the schema, we first chalk out the key requirements and entities for AlphaProject and before doing that, let us assume that AlphaProject is some project management application having following features:

- User management
- Project tracking
- Task assignment and status updates
- Time tracking

Identify Entities

Identify the main entities involved in the application. For AlphaProject, the primary entities are:

- Users
- Projects
- Tasks
- TimeEntries

Define Tables and Columns

Based on the identified entities, define the tables and their columns. The **users** table will store information about the application's users.

```
CREATE TABLE users (
 id SERIAL PRIMARY KEY,
 username VARCHAR(50) UNIQUE NOT NULL,
 password VARCHAR(255) NOT NULL,
 email VARCHAR(100) UNIQUE NOT NULL,
 created_at TIMESTAMP DEFAULT CURRENT_TIMESTAMP
);
```

The **projects** table will store information about projects managed within the application.

```
CREATE TABLE projects (
 id SERIAL PRIMARY KEY,
```

```
 name VARCHAR(100) NOT NULL,
 description TEXT,
 start_date DATE,
 end_date DATE,
 created_by INT REFERENCES users(id),
 created_at TIMESTAMP DEFAULT CURRENT_TIMESTAMP
);
```

The **tasks** table will store information about tasks associated with projects.

```
CREATE TABLE tasks (
 id SERIAL PRIMARY KEY,
 project_id INT REFERENCES projects(id),
 name VARCHAR(100) NOT NULL,
 description TEXT,
 status VARCHAR(20) DEFAULT 'pending',
 assigned_to INT REFERENCES users(id),
 due_date DATE,
 created_at TIMESTAMP DEFAULT CURRENT_TIMESTAMP
);
```

The **time_entries** table will track the time spent on tasks.

```
CREATE TABLE time_entries (
```

```
 id SERIAL PRIMARY KEY,
 task_id INT REFERENCES tasks(id),
 user_id INT REFERENCES users(id),
 hours DECIMAL(5, 2) NOT NULL,
 entry_date DATE NOT NULL,
 created_at TIMESTAMP DEFAULT CURRENT_TIMESTAMP
);
```

Define Relationships

Establish relationships between the tables using foreign keys. For example:

- Each task is linked to a project through the **project_id** foreign key.
- Each task can be assigned to a user through the **assigned_to** foreign key.
- Each time entry is linked to a task and a user through **task_id** and **user_id** foreign keys.

Define Constraints

Add constraints to ensure data integrity and consistency. Common constraints include **`PRIMARY KEY`**, **`UNIQUE`**, **`NOT NULL`**, and **`FOREIGN KEY`**. For example, if we want to ensure that email addresses are unique:

```
ALTER TABLE users
ADD CONSTRAINT unique_email UNIQUE (email);
```

Indexing

Create indexes to improve query performance. Indexes are typically created on columns frequently used in search conditions or join operations. Let us say we want to create an index on the **`username`** column for faster lookups:

```
CREATE INDEX idx_users_username ON users(username);
```

Create an index on the **`project_id`** column in the **`tasks`** table for faster access to tasks by project:

```
CREATE INDEX idx_tasks_project_id ON tasks(project_id);
```

Sample Program: Creating Database Schema for AlphaProject

Now that we have the plan, we shall build the AlphaProject database schema. Ensure you are logged in as the PostgreSQL user and connected to the **alphaproject_db** database:

```
$ sudo -i -u postgres

$ psql
```

Create the database if it hasn't been created yet:

```
CREATE DATABASE alphaproject_db;

\c alphaproject_db
```

Execute the SQL commands to create the **users**, **projects**, **tasks**, and **time_entries** tables. Then, create Users Table:

```
CREATE TABLE users (

 id SERIAL PRIMARY KEY,

 username VARCHAR(50) UNIQUE NOT NULL,

 password VARCHAR(255) NOT NULL,

 email VARCHAR(100) UNIQUE NOT NULL,

 created_at TIMESTAMP DEFAULT CURRENT_TIMESTAMP

);
```

Create Projects Table:

```
CREATE TABLE projects (
```

```
 id SERIAL PRIMARY KEY,
 name VARCHAR(100) NOT NULL,
 description TEXT,
 start_date DATE,
 end_date DATE,
 created_by INT REFERENCES users(id),
 created_at TIMESTAMP DEFAULT CURRENT_TIMESTAMP
);
```

Create Tasks Table:

```
CREATE TABLE tasks (
 id SERIAL PRIMARY KEY,
 project_id INT REFERENCES projects(id),
 name VARCHAR(100) NOT NULL,
 description TEXT,
 status VARCHAR(20) DEFAULT 'pending',
 assigned_to INT REFERENCES users(id),
 due_date DATE,
 created_at TIMESTAMP DEFAULT CURRENT_TIMESTAMP
);
```

Create TimeEntries Table:

```
CREATE TABLE time_entries (
```

```
  id SERIAL PRIMARY KEY,
  task_id INT REFERENCES tasks(id),
  user_id INT REFERENCES users(id),
  hours DECIMAL(5, 2) NOT NULL,
  entry_date DATE NOT NULL,
  created_at TIMESTAMP DEFAULT CURRENT_TIMESTAMP
);
```

Create indexes to enhance performance.

```
CREATE INDEX idx_users_username ON users(username);
CREATE INDEX idx_tasks_project_id ON tasks(project_id);
```

Verify that the tables and indexes have been created correctly by querying the database:

```
\d
```

This command will list all tables, and **`\d table_name`** will show details for a specific table.

Database Integration with AlphaProject

Now that the database schema is in place, you can integrate it with the AlphaProject application. Ensure your application uses the correct connection settings and performs necessary database operations like creating, reading, updating, and deleting records.

For example, in a Python application using SQLAlchemy:

```
from sqlalchemy import create_engine
from sqlalchemy.ext.declarative import declarative_base
from sqlalchemy.orm import sessionmaker
```

```
DATABASE_URL =
"postgresql://alphaproject_user:yourpassword@localhost/al
phaproject_db"


engine = create_engine(DATABASE_URL)

SessionLocal = sessionmaker(autocommit=False,
autoflush=False, bind=engine)

Base = declarative_base()
```

Define models that map to your database tables:

```
from sqlalchemy import Column, Integer, String, Text,
ForeignKey, Date, DECIMAL, TIMESTAMP

from sqlalchemy.orm import relationship


class User(Base):

 __tablename__ = 'users'


 id = Column(Integer, primary_key=True, index=True)

 username = Column(String(50), unique=True,
nullable=False)

 password = Column(String(255), nullable=False)

 email = Column(String(100), unique=True, nullable=False)

 created_at = Column(TIMESTAMP, default='now()')
```

```
class Project(Base):
 __tablename__ = 'projects'

 id = Column(Integer, primary_key=True, index=True)
 name = Column(String(100), nullable=False)
 description = Column(Text)
 start_date = Column(Date)
 end_date = Column(Date)
 created_by = Column(Integer, ForeignKey('users.id'))
 created_at = Column(TIMESTAMP, default='now()')
 user = relationship('User')

class Task(Base):
 __tablename__ = 'tasks'

 id = Column(Integer, primary_key=True, index=True)
 project_id = Column(Integer, ForeignKey('projects.id'))
 name = Column(String(100), nullable=False)
 description = Column(Text)
 status = Column(String(20), default='pending')
 assigned_to = Column(Integer, ForeignKey('users.id'))
```

```
    due_date = Column(Date)
    created_at = Column(TIMESTAMP, default='now()')
    project = relationship('Project')
    user = relationship('User')


class TimeEntry(Base):
    __tablename__ = 'time_entries'


    id = Column(Integer, primary_key=True, index=True)
    task_id = Column(Integer, ForeignKey('tasks.id'))
    user_id = Column(Integer, ForeignKey('users.id'))
    hours = Column(DECIMAL(5, 2), nullable=False)
    entry_date = Column(Date, nullable=False)
    created_at = Column(TIMESTAMP, default='now()')
    task = relationship('Task')
    user = relationship('User')
```

That way, AlphaProject can keep its data organized, which will help it meet the needs of the application while also protecting its integrity and speeding up its operations. This structured approach lays the groundwork for developing and scaling the application.

Performing Database Migrations

The management of data and schema changes throughout time necessitates database migrations. Developers can use them to apply updates in stages, make sure everything is consistent across environments, and upgrade or transfer databases with ease. Here, we will show you how to use a tool that makes database migrations easier, explain why they're necessary, and go over some practical steps to migrate your databases.

Why Database Migration?

Database migrations are crucial for several reasons:

- As applications evolve, the database schema must also adapt to accommodate new features, improve performance, or correct design flaws.
- Migrations enable tracking of database changes over time, ensuring that all environments (development, testing, production) remain consistent.
- Migrations provide mechanisms to revert changes if necessary, ensuring data integrity and reducing downtime during updates.
- Migrations facilitate collaboration among team members by providing a clear history of database changes and allowing multiple developers to work on the same database schema.

Installing and Setting up Alembic

Alembic is a lightweight database migration tool for use with SQLAlchemy, the database toolkit and ORM for Python. Alembic is designed to work with databases supported by SQLAlchemy, including PostgreSQL. It provides a straightforward way to manage database schema changes through versioned migration scripts.

Let us now look at getting this Alembic feed into our system:

Install Alembic

First, install Alembic using pip:

```
$ pip install alembic
```

Initialize Alembic

Navigate to your project directory and initialize Alembic:

```
$ alembic init alembic
```

This command creates an **alembic** directory and a configuration file **alembic.ini**.

Configure Alembic

Edit the **alembic.ini** file to configure the database connection string:

```
[alembic]
# path to migration scripts
script_location = alembic

[loggers]
keys = root,sqlalchemy,alembic

[handlers]
keys = console

[formatters]
keys = generic

[logger_root]
level = WARN
handlers = console
qualname =

[logger_sqlalchemy]
level = WARN
handlers =
```

```
qualname = sqlalchemy.engine
propagate = 0

[logger_alembic]
level = INFO
handlers =
qualname = alembic
propagate = 0

[handler_console]
class = StreamHandler
args = (sys.stderr,)
level = NOTSET
formatter = generic

[formatter_generic]
format = %(asctime)s %(levelname)-5.5s [%(name)s]
%(message)s

sqlalchemy.url =
postgresql://alphaproject_user:yourpassword@localhost/alp
haproject_db
```

Edit the Environment Script

Update the **alembic/env.py** file to connect Alembic with the SQLAlchemy models:

```
from sqlalchemy import engine_from_config, pool
from logging.config import fileConfig
from alembic import context

# Import your SQLAlchemy models
from your_project.models import Base

# this is the Alembic Config object, which provides
# access to the values within the .ini file in use.
config = context.config

# Interpret the config file for Python logging.
# This line sets up loggers basically.
fileConfig(config.config_file_name)

# add your model's MetaData object here
# for 'autogenerate' support
target_metadata = Base.metadata
```

```
def run_migrations_offline():
 """Run migrations in 'offline' mode."""
 url = config.get_main_option("sqlalchemy.url")
 context.configure(url=url,
target_metadata=target_metadata, literal_binds=True)

 with context.begin_transaction():
 context.run_migrations()

def run_migrations_online():
 """Run migrations in 'online' mode."""
 connectable = engine_from_config(
 config.get_section(config.config_ini_section),
 prefix="sqlalchemy.",
 poolclass=pool.NullPool)

 with connectable.connect() as connection:
 context.configure(connection=connection,
target_metadata=target_metadata)

 with context.begin_transaction():
 context.run_migrations()
```

```
if context.is_offline_mode():
 run_migrations_offline()
else:
 run_migrations_online()
```

Creating and Applying Migrations

Create a New Migration

Generate a new migration script:

```
$ alembic revision --autogenerate -m "Initial migration"
```

This command creates a new migration script in the **alembic/versions** directory. The script will include the necessary changes to apply to the database schema based on the current state of the SQLAlchemy models.

Edit the Migration Script

Review and edit the generated migration script if necessary. The script will have **upgrade** and **downgrade** functions to apply and revert changes.

Following is the sample migration script:

```
"""Initial migration


Revision ID: 1234567890ab

Revises:

Create Date: 2024-05-28 12:00:00.000000
```

```
"""
from alembic import op
import sqlalchemy as sa


# revision identifiers, used by Alembic.
revision = '1234567890ab'
down_revision = None
branch_labels = None
depends_on = None


def upgrade():
 # ### commands auto generated by Alembic - please
adjust! ###
 op.create_table('users',
 sa.Column('id', sa.Integer(), nullable=False),
 sa.Column('username', sa.String(length=50),
nullable=False),
 sa.Column('password', sa.String(length=255),
nullable=False),
 sa.Column('email', sa.String(length=100),
nullable=False),
 sa.Column('created_at', sa.TIMESTAMP(),
server_default=sa.func.now(), nullable=True),
```

```
 sa.PrimaryKeyConstraint('id'),
 sa.UniqueConstraint('email'),
 sa.UniqueConstraint('username')
 )
 op.create_table('projects',
 sa.Column('id', sa.Integer(), nullable=False),
 sa.Column('name', sa.String(length=100),
nullable=False),
 sa.Column('description', sa.Text(), nullable=True),
 sa.Column('start_date', sa.Date(), nullable=True),
 sa.Column('end_date', sa.Date(), nullable=True),
 sa.Column('created_by', sa.Integer(), nullable=True),
 sa.Column('created_at', sa.TIMESTAMP(),
server_default=sa.func.now(), nullable=True),
 sa.ForeignKeyConstraint(['created_by'], ['users.id'], ),
 sa.PrimaryKeyConstraint('id')
 )
 # Additional tables and constraints...
 # ### end Alembic commands ###


def downgrade():
```

```
 # ### commands auto generated by Alembic - please
adjust! ###
 op.drop_table('projects')
 op.drop_table('users')
 # ### end Alembic commands ###
```

Apply the Migration

Apply the migration to the database:

```
$ alembic upgrade head
```

This command updates the database schema to match the current state of the models.

Migrating Databases between Systems

To migrate the database to an external system, first, export the current database:

```
$ pg_dump -U alphaproject_user -h localhost -F c -b -v -f
/path/to/backup/alphaproject_db.backup alphaproject_db
```

This command creates a backup file in the custom format. Then, transfer the backup file to the external system using a secure method such as **scp**:

```
$ scp /path/to/backup/alphaproject_db.backup
user@external_system:/path/to/destination
```

On the external system, restore the database from the backup file:

```
$ pg_restore -U alphaproject_user -h localhost -d
alphaproject_db -v
/path/to/destination/alphaproject_db.backup
```

This command restores the database to the external system.

Sample Program: Migrating Database of AlphaProject

Let us demonstrate the entire process wherein we migrate databases of AlphaProject.

After making changes to the models, generate a new migration script:

```
$ alembic revision --autogenerate -m "Add tasks table"
```

Apply the migration to update the database schema:

```
$ alembic upgrade head
```

Export the updated database:

```
$ pg_dump -U alphaproject_user -h localhost -F c -b -v -f
/path/to/backup/alphaproject_db.backup alphaproject_db
```

Transfer the backup file to the external system and restore it:

```
$ scp /path/to/backup/alphaproject_db.backup
user@external_system:/path/to/destination

$ pg_restore -U alphaproject_user -h localhost -d
alphaproject_db -v
/path/to/destination/alphaproject_db.backup
```

After completing these steps, you will be able to migrate databases using Alembic and PostgreSQL with ease. In addition to making upgrades and system transfers easier, this also makes sure that your database schema is consistent across all of your environments.

Backup and Restore Procedures

The availability and integrity of data depends on regular database backups and restorations. With PostgreSQL as our primary focus, this part will teach the various Linux utilities and tools that can be used for backup and restore tasks. Then, we will demonstrate how to practically perform backup and restore operations for the PostgreSQL database used in AlphaProject.

'pg_dump' and 'pg_restore' for Backup and Restore

pg_dump and pg_restore are the primary utilities provided by PostgreSQL for backup and restore operations. These tools are versatile, supporting various backup formats and allowing for both full and partial backups of the database. Pg_dump is used for backing up a PostgreSQL database into a file, and pg_restore is used for restoring a PostgreSQL database from a backup file created by pg_dump itself.

Performing Backup

Install PostgreSQL Tools

Ensure that PostgreSQL and its tools are installed on your system:

```
$ sudo apt update

$ sudo apt install postgresql postgresql-contrib
```

Backup the Database

Use pg_dump to create a backup of the PostgreSQL database. There are different backup formats available:

1. Plain SQL Script: This format creates a SQL script file that contains all the SQL commands needed to recreate the database.
2. Custom Format: This format is specific to pg_restore and allows for selective restoration of database objects.
3. Directory Format: This format creates a directory with one file per database object, also allowing selective restoration.

For this example, we will use the custom format to create backup, which provides more flexibility during the restore process as below:

```
$ pg_dump -U alphaproject_user -h localhost -F c -b -v -f
/path/to/backup/alphaproject_db.backup alphaproject_db
```

Wherein,

- -U: Specifies the database user.
- -h: Specifies the host.
- -F c: Specifies the custom format.
- -b: Includes large objects in the dump.
- -v: Enables verbose mode.
- -f: Specifies the output file.

Verify the Backup

To ensure the backup was successful, check the output file:

```
$ ls -lh /path/to/backup/alphaproject_db.backup
```

Performing Restore Operations

Prepare for Restoration

Before restoring the database, you may need to drop the existing database or ensure the target database is ready for the restore operation.

```
$ psql -U postgres -c "DROP DATABASE IF EXISTS
alphaproject_db;"
```

Create a new database:

```
$ psql -U postgres -c "CREATE DATABASE alphaproject_db
WITH OWNER alphaproject_user;"
```

Restore the Database

Use pg_restore to restore the database from the backup file:

```
$ pg_restore -U alphaproject_user -h localhost -d
alphaproject_db -v /path/to/backup/alphaproject_db.backup
```

Sample Program: Backup and Restore for AlphaProject

Now, let us back up the AlphaProject database using the custom format:

```
$ pg_dump -U alphaproject_user -h localhost -F c -b -v -f
/path/to/backup/alphaproject_db.backup alphaproject_db
```

This command creates a custom-format backup file named **`alphaproject_db.backup`**.

Check that the backup file exists and is not empty:

```
$ ls -lh /path/to/backup/alphaproject_db.backup
```

Drop the existing **alphaproject_db** database and create a new one:

```
$ psql -U postgres -c "DROP DATABASE IF EXISTS
alphaproject_db;"

$ psql -U postgres -c "CREATE DATABASE alphaproject_db
WITH OWNER alphaproject_user;"
```

Restore the database from the backup file using **pg_restore**:

```
$ pg_restore -U alphaproject_user -h localhost -d
alphaproject_db -v /path/to/backup/alphaproject_db.backup
```

This command restores the database schema and data from the backup file into the newly created **alphaproject_db**.

Additional Backup and Restore Options

Incremental Backups

While **pg_dump** and **pg_restore** handle full backups, you can use file system-level backups for incremental backups. Tools like **rsync** can be used to back up only the changed portions of the database files.

Automating Backups

To automate the backup process, you can create a cron job that runs the **pg_dump** command at regular intervals. At first, create a script to perform the backup:

```
$ nano /usr/local/bin/backup_alphaproject.sh
```

Add the following content to the script:

```
#!/bin/bash

TIMESTAMP=$(date +%F)
```

```
BACKUP_DIR="/path/to/backup"

BACKUP_FILE="$BACKUP_DIR/alphaproject_db_$TIMESTAMP.backu
p"


pg_dump -U alphaproject_user -h localhost -F c -b -v -f
$BACKUP_FILE alphaproject_db


# Optional: Remove old backups older than 7 days

find $BACKUP_DIR -type f -name "*.backup" -mtime +7 -exec
rm {} \;
```

Make the script executable:

```
$ chmod +x /usr/local/bin/backup_alphaproject.sh
```

Edit the crontab file to schedule the backup script:

```
$ crontab -e
```

Add the following line to schedule the script to run daily at 2 AM:

```
0 2 * * * /usr/local/bin/backup_alphaproject.sh
```

This quick setup ensures that the AlphaProject database is backed up daily, and old backups are automatically cleaned up.

Monitoring Database Performance with Nagios

The efficiency and capacity of your system to manage the anticipated load can be assured by closely monitoring database performance. To keep tabs on how well your PostgreSQL database is doing, you can set up the robust open-source monitoring tool Nagios. In this section, we will configure Nagios to assess database performance and go over various key performance indicators

(KPIs) to keep track of.

Configuring Nagios to Monitor PostgreSQL

Install PostgreSQL Plugins for Nagios

First, you need to install the necessary PostgreSQL plugins for Nagios. These plugins will allow Nagios to query PostgreSQL and gather performance metrics.

```
$ sudo apt-get install nagios-plugins-contrib
```

Ensure the PostgreSQL plugin (**check_postgres**) is included. If not, you may need to install it separately.

Configure PostgreSQL for Monitoring

Ensure that PostgreSQL is configured to allow connections from the Nagios server. Edit the **pg_hba.conf** file to allow the Nagios user to connect:

```
$ sudo nano /etc/postgresql/12/main/pg_hba.conf
```

Add the following line to allow connections from the Nagios server:

```
host all nagios_user nagios_server_ip/32 md5
```

Restart PostgreSQL to apply the changes:

```
$ sudo systemctl restart postgresql
```

Create a PostgreSQL User for Monitoring

Create a PostgreSQL user specifically for monitoring:

```
$ sudo -i -u postgres

$ psql

CREATE USER nagios_user WITH PASSWORD 'yourpassword';

GRANT CONNECT ON DATABASE alphaproject_db TO nagios_user;
```

```
GRANT USAGE ON SCHEMA public TO nagios_user;

GRANT SELECT ON ALL TABLES IN SCHEMA public TO
nagios_user;

ALTER DEFAULT PRIVILEGES IN SCHEMA public GRANT SELECT ON
TABLES TO nagios_user;

\q
```

Configure Nagios to Use the PostgreSQL Plugin

Edit the Nagios configuration to add commands for monitoring PostgreSQL. Open the **commands.cfg** file:

```
$ sudo nano /usr/local/nagios/etc/objects/commands.cfg
```

Add the following command definition for **check_postgres**:

```
define command {

 command_name check_postgres_connection

 command_line /usr/lib/nagios/plugins/check_postgres --
host=$HOSTADDRESS$ --dbuser=nagios_user --
dbname=alphaproject_db --action=connection

}
```

Define a Service for PostgreSQL Monitoring

Edit the **services.cfg** file to define a new service for monitoring PostgreSQL:

```
$ sudo nano /usr/local/nagios/etc/objects/services.cfg
```

Add the following service definition:

```
define service {
```

```
use generic-service
host_name localhost
service_description PostgreSQL Connection
check_command check_postgres_connection
check_interval 5
retry_interval 1
max_check_attempts 3
check_period 24x7
notification_interval 60
notification_period 24x7
contacts nagiosadmin
}
```

Restart Nagios

Restart Nagios to apply the changes:

```
$ sudo systemctl restart nagios
```

Monitoring Database Performance KPIs

Now that Nagios is configured to monitor PostgreSQL, we shall learn various database performance KPIs and how to monitor them using Nagios.

Connection Time

It measures the time taken to establish a connection to the database. The Nagios command is **check_postgres --action=connection**

Cache Hit Ratio

It is the percentage of times the data is read from the cache rather than the disk and the Nagios

command is **check_postgres --action=cache_hit**
Following is the command definition for cache hit ratio:

```
define command {

 command_name check_postgres_cache_hit

 command_line /usr/lib/nagios/plugins/check_postgres --
host=$HOSTADDRESS$ --dbuser=nagios_user --
dbname=alphaproject_db --action=cache_hit

}
```

And, below is the service definition for cache hit ratio:

```
define service {

 use generic-service

 host_name localhost

 service_description PostgreSQL Cache Hit Ratio

 check_command check_postgres_cache_hit

 check_interval 5

 retry_interval 1

 max_check_attempts 3

 check_period 24x7

 notification_interval 60

 notification_period 24x7

 contacts nagiosadmin

}
```

Locks

It monitors the number of locks on database objects and it can be run with the command as **check_postgres --action=locks.**

Following is the command definition for locks:

```
define command {

 command_name check_postgres_locks

 command_line /usr/lib/nagios/plugins/check_postgres --
host=$HOSTADDRESS$ --dbuser=nagios_user --
dbname=alphaproject_db --action=locks

}
```

And, the service definition for locks is:

```
define service {

 use generic-service

 host_name localhost

 service_description PostgreSQL Locks

 check_command check_postgres_locks

 check_interval 5

 retry_interval 1

 max_check_attempts 3

 check_period 24x7

 notification_interval 60

 notification_period 24x7

 contacts nagiosadmin
```

```
}
```

Disk Usage

This monitors the disk usage of the database through the following command: **check_postgres --action=disk_space.**

Below is the command definition for disk usage:

```
define command {
 command_name check_postgres_disk_space
 command_line /usr/lib/nagios/plugins/check_postgres --
host=$HOSTADDRESS$ --dbuser=nagios_user --
dbname=alphaproject_db --action=disk_space
}
```

And the service definition for disk usage is:

```
define service {
 use generic-service
 host_name localhost
 service_description PostgreSQL Disk Usage
 check_command check_postgres_disk_space
 check_interval 5
 retry_interval 1
 max_check_attempts 3
 check_period 24x7
 notification_interval 60
```

```
 notification_period 24x7
 contacts nagiosadmin
}
```

Replication Lag

This command monitors the replication lag in a master-slave setup with the following command: **check_postgres --action=repl_lag.**

Below is the command definition for replication lag:

```
define command {
 command_name check_postgres_repl_lag
 command_line /usr/lib/nagios/plugins/check_postgres --
host=$HOSTADDRESS$ --dbuser=nagios_user --
dbname=alphaproject_db --action=repl_lag
}
```

And, the service definition for replication lag is as below:

```
define service {
 use generic-service
 host_name localhost
 service_description PostgreSQL Replication Lag
 check_command check_postgres_repl_lag
 check_interval 5
 retry_interval 1
 max_check_attempts 3
```

```
    check_period 24x7
    notification_interval 60
    notification_period 24x7
    contacts nagiosadmin
}
```

By configuring Nagios with these commands and services, you can effectively track critical performance metrics for your PostgreSQL database in AlphaProject. If you set it up this way, you will be notified when there is a performance problem and can take preventative actions to keep your database running well.

Securing Database Systems

Overview

Securing database systems is essential to protect sensitive data from unauthorized access and potential breaches. Database security involves implementing measures to safeguard data, control access, and ensure that only authorized users can perform specific actions. This includes setting up proper authentication, managing access permissions, encrypting data, and monitoring for suspicious activities.

Authentication and Access Control

Strong Password Policies

Ensure all users have strong passwords. PostgreSQL can enforce password policies through **pg_hba.conf**.

Edit the **pg_hba.conf** file to require password authentication:

```
$ sudo nano /etc/postgresql/12/main/pg_hba.conf
```

Ensure the following entries use **md5** or **scram-sha-256** for secure password hashing:

```
host all all 127.0.0.1/32 scram-sha-256
```

```
host all all ::1/128 scram-sha-256
```

Restart the PostgreSQL service to apply the changes:

```
$ sudo systemctl restart postgresql
```

Role-Based Access Control

Create roles with specific privileges and assign users to these roles.

```
CREATE ROLE read_only;

GRANT CONNECT ON DATABASE alphaproject_db TO read_only;

GRANT USAGE ON SCHEMA public TO read_only;

GRANT SELECT ON ALL TABLES IN SCHEMA public TO read_only;

ALTER DEFAULT PRIVILEGES IN SCHEMA public GRANT SELECT ON
TABLES TO read_only;
```

Assign Users to the Role

```
GRANT read_only TO some_user;
```

Network Security

Configuring Firewall

Use **iptables** or **ufw** to restrict access to the PostgreSQL server. To limit PostgreSQL to accept connections only from the localhost:

```
$ sudo ufw allow from 127.0.0.1 to any port 5432
```

SSL/TLS Encryption

Encrypt traffic between the PostgreSQL server and clients to protect data in transit. Generate a self-signed SSL certificate and key:

```
$ sudo openssl req -new -x509 -days 365 -nodes -out
/etc/ssl/certs/postgresql.crt -keyout
/etc/ssl/private/postgresql.key

$ sudo chmod 600 /etc/ssl/private/postgresql.key
```

Configure PostgreSQL to Use SSL by editing the **`postgresql.conf`** file to enable SSL:

```
$ sudo nano /etc/postgresql/12/main/postgresql.conf
```

Ensure the following settings are configured:

```
ssl = on

ssl_cert_file = '/etc/ssl/certs/postgresql.crt'

ssl_key_file = '/etc/ssl/private/postgresql.key'
```

Restart the PostgreSQL service:

```
$ sudo systemctl restart postgresql
```

Data Encryption

Encrypting Data at Rest

Encrypt the database files on disk to protect data if the physical storage is compromised. Use LUKS (Linux Unified Key Setup) to encrypt the file system where PostgreSQL data is stored.

```
$ sudo cryptsetup luksFormat /dev/sdX

$ sudo cryptsetup luksOpen /dev/sdX encrypted_data

$ sudo mkfs.ext4 /dev/mapper/encrypted_data

$ sudo mount /dev/mapper/encrypted_data
/var/lib/postgresql
```

Column-Level Encryption

Use PostgreSQL's built-in functions or extensions to encrypt specific columns. Install the **pgcrypto** extension if not already installed:

```
$ sudo -u postgres psql -c "CREATE EXTENSION pgcrypto;"
```

Encrypt sensitive data when inserting:

```
INSERT INTO users (username, password, email)

VALUES ('john_doe', crypt('password123', gen_salt('bf')),
'john.doe@gitforgits.com');
```

Decrypt data when querying:

```
SELECT username, email, (password = crypt('password123',
password)) AS password_match

FROM users

WHERE username = 'john_doe';
```

Monitoring and Auditing

Logging

Enable detailed logging to track access and changes to the database. Edit the **postgresql.conf** file to configure logging:

```
$ sudo nano /etc/postgresql/12/main/postgresql.conf
```

Set the following parameters:

```
logging_collector = on

log_directory = 'pg_log'

log_filename = 'postgresql-%a.log'
```

```
log_statement = 'all'

log_duration = on
```

Restart the PostgreSQL service:

```
$ sudo systemctl restart postgresql
```

Using Audit Extensions

Install and configure audit extensions such as **pgaudit** to monitor and log database activities.

Install the **pgaudit** extension:

```
$ sudo apt-get install postgresql-12-pgaudit
```

Edit the **postgresql.conf** file to load the **pgaudit** extension and configure auditing:

```
$ sudo nano /etc/postgresql/12/main/postgresql.conf
```

Add the following lines:

```
shared_preload_libraries = 'pgaudit'

pgaudit.log = 'all'
```

Restart the PostgreSQL service:

```
$ sudo systemctl restart postgresql
```

Regular Security Updates

Keeping PostgreSQL Updated

Ensure PostgreSQL is regularly updated to include the latest security patches by updating the Package List.

```
$ sudo apt update
```

Upgrade PostgreSQL as below:

```
$ sudo apt upgrade postgresql
```

Automating Updates

Automate security updates using **unattended-upgrades.** To do this, first install **unattended-upgrades**.

```
$ sudo apt-get install unattended-upgrades
```

Edit the configuration file to enable automatic updates:

```
$ sudo nano /etc/apt/apt.conf.d/50unattended-upgrades
```

Ensure the following lines are uncommented:

```
"${distro_id}:${distro_codename}-updates";

"${distro_id}:${distro_codename}-security";
```

Enable unattended upgrades:

```
$ sudo dpkg-reconfigure --priority=low unattended-
upgrades
```

Sample Program: Securing PostgreSQL for AlphaProject

Let us implement the discussed security measures for the AlphaProject PostgreSQL database. First, ensure **pg_hba.conf** uses secure password hashing:

```
host all all 127.0.0.1/32 scram-sha-256

host all all ::1/128 scram-sha-256
```

Generate SSL certificates and configure PostgreSQL to use them:

```
$ sudo openssl req -new -x509 -days 365 -nodes -out
/etc/ssl/certs/postgresql.crt -keyout
/etc/ssl/private/postgresql.key

$ sudo chmod 600 /etc/ssl/private/postgresql.key


$ sudo nano /etc/postgresql/12/main/postgresql.conf

ssl = on

ssl_cert_file = '/etc/ssl/certs/postgresql.crt'

ssl_key_file = '/etc/ssl/private/postgresql.key'
```

Restart PostgreSQL:

```
$ sudo systemctl restart postgresql
```

Configure PostgreSQL logging:

```
logging_collector = on

log_directory = 'pg_log'

log_filename = 'postgresql-%a.log'

log_statement = 'all'

log_duration = on
```

Restart PostgreSQL:

```
$ sudo systemctl restart postgresql
```

Install and configure **pgaudit**:

```
$ sudo apt-get install postgresql-12-pgaudit
```

```
$ sudo nano /etc/postgresql/12/main/postgresql.conf

shared_preload_libraries = 'pgaudit'

pgaudit.log = 'all'

$ sudo systemctl restart postgresql
```

The data stored in AlphaProject will be safe and secure from any dangers that may arise as a result of these security measures being put into place.

Automating Database Operations

The management of databases can be made much more efficient, error-free, and consistent with the help of automation. In this section, we will go over everything needed to automate the PostgreSQL database's provisioning, backups, restores, updates, and caching in AlphaProject.

Automating Database Provisioning

Provisioning involves setting up a new database instance and configuring it for use. Automation tools like Ansible can be used to script the entire provisioning process.

Install Ansible

Ensure Ansible is installed on your system:

```
$ sudo apt update

$ sudo apt install ansible
```

Create an Ansible Playbook

Create a playbook to automate the provisioning of a PostgreSQL database.

```
$ nano provision_postgresql.yml
```

Add the following content to the playbook:

```
---
```

```
- name: Provision PostgreSQL Database
 hosts: db_servers
 become: yes
 tasks:
 - name: Install PostgreSQL
 apt:
 name: postgresql
 state: present
 update_cache: yes

 - name: Install PostgreSQL Contrib
 apt:
 name: postgresql-contrib
 state: present

 - name: Ensure PostgreSQL service is running
 service:
 name: postgresql
 state: started
 enabled: true
```

```
- name: Create PostgreSQL user

become_user: postgres

postgresql_user:

name: alphaproject_user

password: yourpassword

state: present


- name: Create PostgreSQL database

become_user: postgres

postgresql_db:

name: alphaproject_db

owner: alphaproject_user

state: present
```

Run the Playbook

Execute the playbook to provision the PostgreSQL database:

```
$ ansible-playbook -i inventory provision_postgresql.yml
```

This playbook installs PostgreSQL, starts the service, creates a user, and sets up the database.

Automating Backups and Restores

Automating backups and restores ensures that data is consistently backed up and can be restored quickly in case of failure. At first, create a script to perform the backup:

```
$ nano backup_postgresql.sh
```

Add the following content:

```
#!/bin/bash

TIMESTAMP=$(date +%F)

BACKUP_DIR="/path/to/backup"

BACKUP_FILE="$BACKUP_DIR/alphaproject_db_$TIMESTAMP.backu
p"


pg_dump -U alphaproject_user -h localhost -F c -b -v -f
$BACKUP_FILE alphaproject_db


# Optional: Remove old backups older than 7 days

find $BACKUP_DIR -type f -name "*.backup" -mtime +7 -exec
rm {} \;
```

Make the script executable:

```
$ chmod +x backup_postgresql.sh
```

Edit the crontab file to schedule the backup script:

```
$ crontab -e
```

Add the following line to schedule the script to run daily at 2 AM:

```
0 2 * * * /path/to/backup_postgresql.sh
```

Create a script to restore the database:

```
$ nano restore_postgresql.sh
```

Add the following content:

```
#!/bin/bash

BACKUP_FILE="/path/to/backup/alphaproject_db_latest.backu
p"


# Drop the existing database

psql -U postgres -c "DROP DATABASE IF EXISTS
alphaproject_db;"


# Create a new database

psql -U postgres -c "CREATE DATABASE alphaproject_db WITH
OWNER alphaproject_user;"


# Restore the database

pg_restore -U alphaproject_user -h localhost -d
alphaproject_db -v $BACKUP_FILE
```

Make the script executable:

```
$ chmod +x restore_postgresql.sh
```

Automating Updates

Automate the process of applying updates to ensure the database is always running the latest version.

First, create a script to update PostgreSQL:

```
$ nano update_postgresql.sh
```

Add the following content:

```
#!/bin/bash

# Update package list

sudo apt update


# Upgrade PostgreSQL

sudo apt upgrade -y postgresql
```

Make the script executable:

```
$ chmod +x update_postgresql.sh
```

Edit the crontab file to schedule the update script:

```
$ crontab -e
```

Add the following line to schedule the script to run weekly at 3 AM on Sundays:

```
0 3 * * 0 /path/to/update_postgresql.sh
```

Automating Database Caching

Database caching improves performance by storing frequently accessed data in memory. Tools like Redis can be used to cache database queries.

First, install Redis on your system:

```
$ sudo apt update

$ sudo apt install redis-server
```

Modify your application to use Redis for caching database queries. For example, in a Python application using SQLAlchemy and Flask:

```
$ pip install Flask-Caching redis
```

Add the following configuration to your Flask application:

```
from flask import Flask

from flask_caching import Cache

from sqlalchemy import create_engine


app = Flask(__name__)

app.config['CACHE_TYPE'] = 'redis'

app.config['CACHE_REDIS_HOST'] = 'localhost'

app.config['CACHE_REDIS_PORT'] = 6379

app.config['CACHE_REDIS_DB'] = 0

app.config['CACHE_REDIS_URL'] =
'redis://localhost:6379/0'


cache = Cache(app)


engine =
create_engine('postgresql://alphaproject_user:yourpasswor
d@localhost/alphaproject_db')


@app.route('/cached_query')

@cache.cached(timeout=60)
```

```
def cached_query():
 with engine.connect() as connection:
 result = connection.execute("SELECT * FROM some_table
LIMIT 10")
 return str(list(result))
```

This configuration sets up Flask-Caching to use Redis and caches the result of the **cached_query** endpoint for 60 seconds. These automation scripts and configurations reduce the need for manual intervention, minimize the risk of errors, and help maintain a robust and reliable database system.

Summary

This chapter covered the fundamentals of database management in a Linux environment with an emphasis on PostgreSQL for AlphaProject. In the first part of the chapter, we learned about Linux databases and how PostgreSQL works, with an emphasis on how it is better than competing systems like Windows in terms of performance. The installation and configuration of PostgreSQL were covered in detail, allowing users to easily set up a powerful database system. It was shown how to build a database schema for AlphaProject, including how to define associations, create tables, and put constraints in place to keep data efficient and accurate.

We then moved on to learn about database migrations and how to execute them, stressing how crucial they are for schema evolution and version control. You learnt how to easily manage updates and automate changes to database schemas using the Alembic tool. After that, the steps to take for backing up and restoring data were explained in detail with examples of how to utilize pg_dump and pg_restore to protect data and guarantee a speedy recovery in the event of accidents. Also included were scripts and scheduling methods for automated restores and backups.

You were then shown how to set up Nagios to monitor critical performance indicators such as replication lag, disk use, connection time, cache hit ratio, locks, and cache hit ratio, among others, as the chapter progressed. Password rules, SSL/TLS encryption, role-based access control, and complete logging and auditing using tools like pgaudit were all important parts of the learnings on securing the PostgreSQL database.

In the end, we covered database automation, showing you how to use Ansible for provisioning, write scripts to perform backups, restorations, and updates regularly, and integrate Redis for database caching. Efficiency, consistency, and reliability in database management were the goals of these automation systems, which sought to decrease the need for human intervention. To sum up, this chapter has given us the tools we need to operate PostgreSQL databases safely and efficiently on Linux.

CHAPTER 5: SYSTEM HEALTH MONITORING

Introduction

In Chapter 5, "System Health Monitoring," you will delve into crucial techniques and tools for maintaining the optimal performance and reliability of Linux systems. This chapter begins with monitoring CPU and memory usage, providing insights into how to track and manage system resources effectively to prevent bottlenecks and ensure smooth operation. Disk space monitoring and management will be covered next, teaching how to keep track of disk usage and avoid issues related to insufficient storage.

The chapter will also focus on tracking network performance, an essential aspect of system health monitoring, to ensure that network traffic is flowing efficiently without interruptions or slowdowns. Readers will learn to use powerful tools like **`top`** and **`htop`** for real-time system monitoring, offering a user-friendly way to observe various system metrics. Additionally, monitoring with Nagios and Zabbix will be explored, highlighting how these tools can be used to provide comprehensive monitoring solutions and keep systems running optimally.

Setting up alerts and notifications is another critical topic, enabling administrators to respond promptly to any issues or anomalies. Analyzing system logs will teach you to interpret log files and diagnose potential problems. Performance tuning will walkthrough us through fine-tuning system settings for improved performance, while maintaining system uptime will focus on strategies to keep systems operational with minimal downtime. Finally, capacity planning will be learned, providing techniques to anticipate future resource needs and ensure systems can handle growth and increased demand. This chapter aims to equip you with the knowledge and skills needed to monitor and maintain the health of your Linux systems effectively.

Monitoring CPU and Memory Usage

Overview

Monitoring CPU and memory usage is vital for system administrators to ensure the smooth operation of Linux systems. It involves tracking how system resources are utilized and identifying potential performance bottlenecks. Following are the key Infrastructure Resources monitored by Sysadmins:

- CPU Usage: The percentage of the CPU being used by processes. High CPU usage can indicate heavy workloads or inefficient processes.
- Memory Usage: The amount of RAM being used by the system. Monitoring memory helps prevent issues like swapping, which can degrade performance.
- Disk I/O: The rate at which data is read from or written to disk. High disk I/O can be a bottleneck, especially for applications requiring fast data access.
- Network Usage: The amount of data being transmitted and received over network interfaces. Monitoring network traffic helps identify bandwidth issues and potential

bottlenecks.

In this section, we will learn the key infrastructure resources monitored by sysadmins, introduce tools like **vmstat**, and demonstrate how to calculate and monitor usage.

Tools for Monitoring CPU and Memory Usage

vmstat is a versatile tool that provides a snapshot of system performance, including CPU and memory usage. It offers a real-time view of various system metrics and is useful for identifying performance issues. **top** and **htop** are interactive tools that display real-time system information. They provide detailed views of processes, CPU, memory usage, and more. **mpstat** is another tool that provides CPU usage statistics, which can be useful for monitoring multi-processor systems.

Using 'vmstat' to Monitor CPU and Memory Usage

- Ensure **vmstat** is installed on your system:

```
$ sudo apt update $ sudo apt install sysstat
```

- Run **vmstat** to see the output:

```
$ vmstat 5 5
```

- This command runs **vmstat** with a 5-second interval, printing 5 reports.

```
procs -----------memory---------- ---swap-- -----io---- -system-- ------cpu----- r b swpd free buff cache si so bi bo in cs us sy id wa st 1 0 0 12345 6789 12345 0 0 1 2 10 20 5 2 90 3 0
```

- The columns in the output represent various metrics:
  - procs: **r** (processes running), **b** (processes blocked).
  - memory: **swpd** (swap used), **free** (free memory), **buff** (buffer memory), **cache** (cached memory).
  - swap: **si** (swap in), **so** (swap out).
  - io: **bi** (blocks in), **bo** (blocks out).
  - system: **in** (interrupts per second), **cs** (context switches per second).
  - cpu: **us** (user time), **sy** (system time), **id** (idle time), **wa** (wait time), **st** (steal time).
- CPU usage is represented by the **us**, **sy**, **id**, **wa**, and **st** columns. High values in **us**

and **sy** indicate heavy CPU usage by user and system processes, respectively. A high **wa** value indicates significant I/O wait time, which could be a performance bottleneck. Following is the desired output of Analysis:

```
------cpu----- us sy id wa st 5 2 90 3 0
```

In the above given code snippet, the CPU is 90% idle, 5% used by user processes, 2% by system processes, and 3% waiting for I/O operations.

- Memory usage is shown in the **swpd**, **free**, **buff**, and **cache** columns. Monitoring these values helps identify potential memory shortages or inefficiencies. Following is the desired output of Analysis:

```
-----------memory---------- swpd free buff cache 0 12345
6789 12345
```

In the above code, **free** shows the available memory, **buff** the buffer memory, and **cache** the cached memory.

Using 'top' and 'htop' for Real-Time Monitoring

Run **top** to view real-time system performance:

```
$ top
```

The **top** command provides a dynamic view of system performance, displaying processes, CPU, and memory usage. Following is the desired output:

```
top - 15:29:03 up 1:29, 1 user, load average: 0.14, 0.19,
0.21 Tasks: 115 total, 1 running, 114 sleeping, 0
stopped, 0 zombie %Cpu(s): 3.0 us, 1.0 sy, 0.0 ni, 95.0
id, 1.0 wa, 0.0 hi, 0.0 si, 0.0 st KiB Mem : 2048576
total, 198432 free, 543672 used, 1301472 buff/cache KiB
Swap: 2097148 total, 2097148 free, 0 used. 978112 avail
Mem PID USER PR NI VIRT RES SHR S %CPU %MEM TIME+ COMMAND
123 root 20 0 162708 2624 1300 S 0.7 0.1 0:00.32 bash 456
postgres 20 0 262476 11236 9056 S 0.3 0.5 0:02.05
postgres
```

- %Cpu(s): Displays CPU usage by user (**us**), system (**sy**), nice (**ni**), idle (**id**), I/O wait (**wa**), hardware interrupts (**hi**), software interrupts (**si**), and steal time (**st**).
- KiB Mem: Shows total, free, used, and buffer/cache memory.
- KiB Swap: Shows total, free, and used swap memory.
- Processes: Lists active processes, with columns for PID, user, priority, nice value, virtual memory, resident memory, shared memory, state, CPU usage, memory usage, and command.

Then. install **`htop`** for an enhanced, interactive view:

```
$ sudo apt install htop $ htop
```

htop provides a more user-friendly interface with color-coded metrics, making it easier to monitor CPU and memory usage. Following is the desired output:

```
1 [| 1.6%] Tasks: 115, 1 running 2 [ 0.0%] Load average:
0.14 0.19 0.21 Mem[||||| 543M/2.0G] Uptime: 1:30 Swp[
0K/2.0G] PID USER PRI NI VIRT RES SHR S CPU% MEM% TIME+
Command 123 root 20 0 162M 2.5M 1.3M S 0.7 0.1 0:00.32
bash 456 postgres 20 0 262M 11.2M 9.0M S 0.3 0.5 0:02.05
postgres
```

Using 'mpstat' for Detailed CPU Usage

Ensure **`mpstat`** is installed:

```
$ sudo apt install sysstat
```

Run **`mpstat`** to get detailed CPU usage statistics:

```
$ mpstat -P ALL 5 5
```

This command shows CPU usage for all processors every 5 seconds, 5 times. Following is the desired output:

```
11:04:27 AM CPU %usr %nice %sys %iowait %irq %soft %steal
%guest %idle 11:04:32 AM all 1.64 0.00 0.41 0.05 0.00
0.01 0.00 0.00 97.88 11:04:32 AM 0 1.83 0.00 0.46 0.09
0.00 0.01 0.00 0.00 97.61
```

In the above shown output,

- %usr: User CPU time.
- %nice: Nice CPU time.
- %sys: System CPU time.
- %iowait: I/O wait time.
- %irq: Hardware interrupt time.
- %soft: Software interrupt time.
- %steal: Steal time.
- %guest: Guest time.
- %idle: Idle time.

Sample Program: Monitoring AlphaProject's System Resources

We shall monitor the CPU and memory usage for AlphaProject using **vmstat**, **top**, **htop**, and **mpstat**.

- Run **vmstat** to monitor system resources:

```
$ vmstat 5 5
```

- Analyze the output to identify CPU and memory usage patterns.
- Run **top** for a real-time view:

```
$ top
```

- Observe processes consuming the most CPU and memory, and identify any potential bottlenecks.
- Run **htop** for an interactive view:

```
$ htop
```

- Use **htop** to navigate and manage processes, providing a clear picture of resource usage.
- Run **mpstat** for detailed CPU usage:

```
$ mpstat -P ALL 5 5
```

- Analyze the output to understand CPU utilization across all processors.

These discussed commands and tools allow system administrators to keep an eye on memory and CPU utilization, which helps keep AlphaProject running smoothly. In order to manage system resources proactively, it is necessary to conduct continuous monitoring in order to detect possible problems early on.

Disk Space Monitoring and Management

Effective disk space monitoring and management are critical for maintaining system performance and avoiding potential issues related to insufficient storage. Following are the key commands for Disk Space Monitoring and Management:

- df: Displays the amount of disk space used and available on file systems.
- du: Estimates file space usage.
- lsblk: Lists information about block devices.
- ncdu: A disk usage analyzer with an ncurses interface (useful for a more interactive experience).

In this section, we will learn key Linux commands like **df** and **du** that are essential for disk space monitoring and management and also learn to use these commands to perform various tasks.

Using 'df' to Monitor Disk Space

df is a straightforward command that provides a summary of disk space usage across all mounted file systems.

- Run df Command (-h: Provides human-readable format (e.g., in GB, MB).

```
$ df -h
```

Following is the desired output:

```
Filesystem Size Used Avail Use% Mounted on udev 1.9G 0
1.9G 0% /dev tmpfs 394M 1.3M 393M 1% /run /dev/sda1 50G
20G 27G 43% / tmpfs 2.0G 25M 2.0G 2% /dev/shm tmpfs 5.0M
0 5.0M 0% /run/lock tmpfs 394M 44K 394M 1% /run/user/1000
```

- Analyze df Output

- Filesystem: The name of each file system.
- Size: Total size of the file system.
- Used: Space used on the file system.
- Avail: Available space on the file system.
- Use%: Percentage of used space.
- Mounted on: The directory where the file system is mounted.

Using 'du' to Estimate File Space Usage

du is used to check the space usage of directories and files.

- Run du Command to get a summary of disk usage in the current directory:
    - -s: Provides a summary for each argument.
    - -h: Provides human-readable format.

```
$ du -sh *
```

Following is the desired output:

```
20M logs 3.1G var 1.2G home 5.5M etc
```

- Analyze du Output

Using 'lsblk' to List Block Devices

lsblk lists information about all available or the specified block devices. It is useful for understanding disk partitioning and usage.

Run lsblk Command

```
$ lsblk
```

Following is the desired output:

```
NAME MAJ:MIN RM SIZE RO TYPE MOUNTPOINT sda 8:0 0 50G 0
disk ├─sda1 8:1 0 50G 0 part / sdb 8:16 0 100G 0 disk
├─sdb1 8:17 0 50G 0 part /data1 ├─sdb2 8:18 0 50G 0 part
/data2
```

- Analyze lsblk Output
    - NAME: Device name.

- SIZE: Size of the device.
- TYPE: Type of the device (disk, part, etc.).
- MOUNTPOINT: Mount point of the device.

Using 'ncdu' for Interactive Disk Usage Analysis

ncdu is a disk usage analyzer with an ncurses interface, providing an interactive way to explore disk usage.

- Install ncdu

```
$ sudo apt install ncdu
```

- Run ncdu

```
$ ncdu /
```

Following is the desired output:

```
4.0 GiB [##########] /usr 1.5 GiB [### ] /var 960.0 MiB
[## ] /home 256.0 MiB [ ] /etc 100.0 MiB [ ] /boot
```

Sample Program: Monitoring and Managing Disk Space in AlpaProject

Example 1: Monitoring Disk Space with 'df'

To monitor the disk space used by AlphaProject, run:

```
$ df -h /var/www/alphaproject
```

Following is the desired output:

```
Filesystem Size Used Avail Use% Mounted on /dev/sda1 50G
30G 18G 63% /var/www/alphaproject
```

This shows that the AlphaProject directory is using 30GB of a 50GB partition, with 18GB available.

Example 2: Checking Directory Sizes with 'du'

To identify which directories within AlphaProject are using the most space:

```
$ du -sh /var/www/alphaproject/*
```

Following is the desired output:

```
200M /var/www/alphaproject/logs 2.5G
/var/www/alphaproject/data 300M
/var/www/alphaproject/uploads
```

This output indicates that the **data** directory is the largest, using 2.5GB.

Example 3: Detailed Analysis with 'du'

For a more detailed look at the **data** directory:

```
$ du -ah /var/www/alphaproject/data
```

Following is the desired output:

```
1.0G /var/www/alphaproject/data/file1.bin 1.5G
/var/www/alphaproject/data/file2.bin 2.5G
/var/www/alphaproject/data
```

This shows the individual file sizes within the **data** directory.

Example 4: Interactive Analysis with 'ncdu'

To use **ncdu** for an interactive analysis of AlphaProject's disk usage:

```
$ ncdu /var/www/alphaproject
```

Navigate through the directories to find the largest files and directories.

To keep AlphaProject from exceeding its storage restrictions and running at peak performance, system administrators must use these commands and tools to properly manage and monitor disk space.

Tracking Network Performance

Overview

Monitoring network performance is crucial for ensuring that applications run smoothly and efficiently. Following are the key commands for Tracking Network Performance:

- ping: Checks the reachability of a host and measures round-trip time for messages sent from the originating host to a destination computer.
- traceroute: Traces the route packets take to reach a network host.
- iftop: Displays bandwidth usage on an interface by host.
- netstat: Displays network connections, routing tables, interface statistics, masquerade connections, and multicast memberships.
- vnstat: A network traffic monitor for logging and analyzing network traffic usage.

In this section, we will learn some of the best Linux commands for tracking network performance, including **`ping`**, **`traceroute`**, **`iftop`**, **`netstat`**, and **`vnstat`**. We will then learn how to use these commands to monitor various aspects of the network performance for AlphaProject.

Using 'ping' to Check Network Connectivity

ping is a basic network utility that tests the reachability of a host on an IP network and measures the round-trip time for messages.

To check the connectivity to a host, run:

```
$ ping www.gitforgits.com
```

Following is the desired output:

```
PING www.gitforgits.com (93.184.216.34): 56 data bytes 64
bytes from 93.184.216.34: icmp_seq=0 ttl=56 time=13.3 ms
64 bytes from 93.184.216.34: icmp_seq=1 ttl=56 time=12.9
ms 64 bytes from 93.184.216.34: icmp_seq=2 ttl=56
time=13.0 ms
```

Wherein,

- icmp_seq: Sequence number of the message.
- ttl: Time to live.
- time: Round-trip time.

This output shows the latency (time) in milliseconds for packets to reach the host and return. Consistently high times or packet loss indicates network issues.

Using 'traceroute' to Trace Network Paths

traceroute shows the path packets take to reach a network host, which helps diagnose routing issues.

Run traceroute Command:

```
$ traceroute www.gitforgits.com
```

Following is the desired output:

```
traceroute to www.gitforgits.com (93.184.216.34), 30 hops
max, 60 byte packets 1 router.local (192.168.1.1) 1.223
ms 1.173 ms 1.157 ms 2 10.0.0.1 (10.0.0.1) 2.432 ms 2.427
ms 2.418 ms 3 172.16.0.1 (172.16.0.1) 15.367 ms 15.337 ms
15.324 ms 4 example.net (93.184.216.34) 13.343 ms 13.320
ms 13.301 ms
```

In the above output, each line shows a hop in the path, including the router IP and round-trip time. Delays or timeouts at specific hops can indicate where issues occur.

Using 'iftop' to Monitor Bandwidth Usage

iftop is a real-time console-based network bandwidth monitoring tool. To begin with, install iftop:

```
$ sudo apt-get install iftop
```

Run iftop command:

```
$ sudo iftop
```

Following is the desired output:

```
interface: eth0 => dst. <= src 192.168.1.2:49152 =>
93.184.216.34:80 4.00Kb 4.00Kb 4.00Kb 192.168.1.2:49152
<= 93.184.216.34:80 3.00Kb 3.00Kb 3.00Kb TX: cum: 4.00Kb
peak: 4.00Kb rates: 4.00Kb 4.00Kb 4.00Kb RX: cum: 3.00Kb
peak: 3.00Kb rates: 3.00Kb 3.00Kb 3.00Kb TOTAL: cum:
7.00Kb peak: 7.00Kb rates: 7.00Kb 7.00Kb 7.00Kb
```

In the above iftop output,

- TX: Transmit rates.
- RX: Receive rates.
- TOTAL: Combined traffic.

This output helps identify which hosts are using the most bandwidth.

Using 'netstat' to Display Network Statistics

netstat provides network statistics and details about network connections.

```
$ netstat -tuln
```

Following is the desired output:

```
Active Internet connections (only servers) Proto Recv-Q
Send-Q Local Address Foreign Address State tcp 0 0
0.0.0.0:22 0.0.0.0:* LISTEN tcp6 0 0 :::80 :::* LISTEN
udp 0 0 0.0.0.0:123 0.0.0.0:* udp6 0 0 :::123 :::*
```

In the above netstat output,

- Proto: Protocol (TCP, UDP).
- Recv-Q: Receive queue.
- Send-Q: Send queue.
- Local Address: Local IP address and port.
- Foreign Address: Remote IP address and port.
- State: Connection state (LISTEN, ESTABLISHED, etc.).

This output shows active connections and listening ports.

Using 'vnstat' to Monitor Network Traffic

vnstat logs network traffic and provides statistics on data usage. To begin with, install vnstat:

```
$ sudo apt-get install vnstat
```

Initialize vnstat database:

```
$ sudo vnstat -u -i eth0
```

Run vnstat command:

```
$ vnstat
```

Following is the desired output:

```
rx / tx / total / estimated eth0: Apr '24 1.95 GiB / 1.23 GiB / 3.18 GiB / 3.51 GiB today 50.34 MiB / 30.20 MiB / 80.54 MiB / 101.2 MiB
```

In the below vnstat output,

- rx: Received data.
- tx: Transmitted data.
- total: Combined traffic.
- estimated: Estimated traffic for the period.

This output provides an overview of network usage over time.

Sample Program: AlphaProject's Network Performance

Example 1: Checking Network Connectivity with 'ping'

To ensure AlphaProject's server can reach the database server:

```
$ ping db-server.gitforgits.com
```

Following is the desired output:

```
PING db-server.gitforgits.com (192.168.1.10): 56 data
bytes 64 bytes from 192.168.1.10: icmp_seq=0 ttl=64
time=0.512 ms 64 bytes from 192.168.1.10: icmp_seq=1
ttl=64 time=0.475 ms
```

Example 2: Tracing Network Path with 'traceroute'

To diagnose routing issues to the web server:

```
$ traceroute web-server.gitforgits.com
```

Following is the desired output:

```
traceroute to web-server.gitforgits.com (192.168.1.20),
30 hops max, 60 byte packets 1 192.168.1.1 (192.168.1.1)
1.223 ms 1.173 ms 1.157 ms 2 10.0.0.1 (10.0.0.1) 2.432 ms
2.427 ms 2.418 ms 3 172.16.0.1 (172.16.0.1) 15.367 ms

web-server.gitforgits.com (192.168.1.20) 13.343 ms 13.320
ms 13.301 ms
```

This output helps identify any delays or issues in the network path.

Example 3: Monitoring Bandwidth Usage with 'iftop'

To monitor real-time bandwidth usage on AlphaProject's network interface:

```
$ sudo iftop -i eth0
```

Following is the desired output:

```
interface: eth0 => dst. <= src 192.168.1.2:49152 =>
93.184.216.34:80 4.00Kb 4.00Kb 4.00Kb 192.168.1.2:49152
<= 93.184.216.34:80 3.00Kb 3.00Kb 3.00Kb TX: cum: 4.00Kb
peak: 4.00Kb rates: 4.00Kb 4.00Kb 4.00Kb RX: cum: 3.00Kb
peak: 3.00Kb rates: 3.00Kb 3.00Kb 3.00Kb TOTAL: cum:
7.00Kb peak: 7.00Kb rates: 7.00Kb 7.00Kb 7.00Kb
```

This output shows which connections are using the most bandwidth, helping to identify potential bottlenecks or unauthorized usage.

Example 4: Displaying Network Statistics with 'netstat'

To view active network connections and listening ports for AlphaProject:

```
$ netstat -tuln
```

Following is the desired output:

```
Active Internet connections (only servers) Proto Recv-Q
Send-Q Local Address Foreign Address State tcp 0 0
0.0.0.0:22 0.0.0.0:* LISTEN tcp6 0 0 :::80 :::* LISTEN
udp 0 0 0.0.0.0:123 0.0.0.0:* udp6 0 0 :::123 :::*
```

This output helps ensure that only the necessary services are running and listening on the expected ports.

Example 5: Monitoring Network Traffic with 'vnstat'

To get an overview of the network traffic usage for AlphaProject over the past month and today:

```
$ vnstat
```

Following is the desired output:

```
rx / tx / total / estimated eth0: Apr '24 1.95 GiB / 1.23
GiB / 3.18 GiB / 3.51 GiB today 50.34 MiB / 30.20 MiB /
80.54 MiB / 101.2 MiB
```

This output provides a clear view of how much data has been transferred over time, helping to identify any unusual spikes in traffic.

With all these commands and tools learned in this section, system administrators may keep tabs on how AlphaProject's network is doing in many areas.

Using 'top' and 'htop' for System Monitoring

System administrators monitor various aspects of a system to ensure its smooth operation and to prevent potential issues. Key aspects include CPU usage, memory usage, disk I/O, network activity, and process management. Monitoring these parameters helps in identifying performance bottlenecks, diagnosing issues, and optimizing system resources.

Following are the key aspects monitored by Sysadmins:

- CPU Usage: Tracks the percentage of CPU being used by processes.
- Memory Usage: Monitors the amount of RAM used, available, and the swap space utilization.
- Disk I/O: Observes the rate of data being read from and written to disk.
- Network Activity: Measures data transmission and reception rates over network interfaces.
- Process Management: Lists active processes, their resource usage, and status.

Using 'top' for System Monitoring

top is a powerful command-line tool that provides a real-time view of system performance, displaying various metrics related to CPU, memory, and processes.

- Run top Command

```
$ top
```

Following is the desired output:

```
top - 10:34:18 up 10 days, 23:17, 1 user, load average:
0.05, 0.11, 0.09 Tasks: 125 total, 1 running, 124
sleeping, 0 stopped, 0 zombie %Cpu(s): 1.0 us, 0.5 sy,
0.0 ni, 98.0 id, 0.5 wa, 0.0 hi, 0.0 si, 0.0 st KiB Mem :
2048576 total, 498072 free, 745392 used, 805112
buff/cache KiB Swap: 2097148 total, 2097148 free, 0 used.
1105160 avail Mem PID USER PR NI VIRT RES SHR S %CPU %MEM
TIME+ COMMAND 897 root 20 0 162708 2624 1300 S 0.7 0.1
0:00.32 bash 1243 postgres 20 0 262476 11236 9056 S 0.3
0.5 0:02.05 postgres
```

In the above top output,

- CPU Usage: **%Cpu(s)** section shows the percentage of CPU time in various states:
- **us** (user): Time spent on user processes.

- **sy** (system): Time spent on system processes.
- **id** (idle): Time when CPU is idle.
- **wa** (iowait): Time spent waiting for I/O operations.
- Memory Usage: **KiB Mem** section shows total, free, used, and buffer/cache memory.
- Swap Usage: **KiB Swap** section shows total, free, and used swap memory.
- Processes: Lists processes with columns for PID, user, priority, nice value, virtual memory, resident memory, shared memory, state, CPU usage, memory usage, and command.

To interact with top:

- Press **q** to quit.
- Press **h** for help.
- Press **M** to sort processes by memory usage.
- Press **P** to sort processes by CPU usage.

Using 'htop' for Enhanced System Monitoring

htop is an interactive process viewer with a more user-friendly interface compared to **top**. It provides a color-coded display of system metrics and allows for easier navigation and process management.

- Install htop

```
$ sudo apt-get install htop
```

- Run htop command

```
$ htop
```

Following is the desired output:

```
1 [| 1.6%] Tasks: 125, 1 running 2 [ 0.0%] Load average:
0.05 0.11 0.09 Mem[||||||||||||||| 745M/2.0G] Uptime: 10
days, 23:17 Swp[ 0K/2.0G] PID USER PRI NI VIRT RES SHR S
CPU% MEM% TIME+ Command 897 root 20 0 162M 2.5M 1.3M S
0.7 0.1 0:00.32 bash 1243 postgres 20 0 262M 11.2M 9.0M S
0.3 0.5 0:02.05 postgres
```

In the above htop output,

- CPU Bars: Display the usage of each CPU core.
- Memory and Swap Bars: Show the current usage of RAM and swap space.
- Load Average: Shows system load averages for the past 1, 5, and 15 minutes.
- Uptime: Indicates how long the system has been running.
- Processes: Lists processes with additional details such as CPU% and MEM% usage.

To interact with htop,

- Press **F6** to sort columns.
- Press **F5** to toggle tree view.
- Press **F9** to kill a process.
- Press **F10** to quit.

Sample Program: Implement System Monitoring

Example 1: Monitoring CPU and Memory Usage with 'top'

Run **`top`** to monitor the overall CPU and memory usage of AlphaProject:

```
$ top
```

Observe the **`%Cpu(s)`** and **`KiB Mem`** sections to ensure that the CPU and memory are not being overutilized. For instance, if the **`us`** or **`sy`** values are consistently high, it might indicate that the system is under heavy load.

Example 2: Identifying High Resource Usage with 'htop'

Run **`htop`** to get a more interactive view of resource usage:

```
$ htop
```

Use the arrow keys to scroll through the list of processes and identify any processes that are consuming an unusually high amount of CPU or memory. For example, if you notice a process using a high percentage of memory, you can further assess that process to determine if it is behaving as expected.

Example 3: Managing Processes with 'top'

If you identify a process that is consuming too many resources and you need to stop it, you can use **`top`** to kill the process:

1. Press **k** within the **top** interface.
2. Enter the PID of the process you want to kill.

3. Confirm by pressing **Enter**.

Example 4: Managing Processes with 'htop'

Similarly, in **`htop`**, you can kill a process more interactively:

1. Press **F9** to kill the process.
2. Select the signal to send (e.g., **SIGKILL**) and press **Enter**.

Example 5: Monitoring Specific Resources

To monitor the CPU usage specifically:

```
$ top -o %CPU
```

To monitor the memory usage specifically:

```
$ top -o %MEM
```

In **`htop`**, press **`F6`** and select **`%CPU`** or **`%MEM`** to sort processes accordingly.

By using **`top`** and **`htop`**, system administrators can effectively monitor and manage the performance of the system running AlphaProject. These tools provide real-time insights into CPU and memory usage, allowing for proactive management of system resources and quick identification of potential performance issues.

Monitoring with Nagios and Zabbix

Introduction to Zabbix

Zabbix is an enterprise-level monitoring platform designed to monitor and track the performance and availability of network servers, devices, and other IT resources. It provides real-time monitoring, data collection, and analysis capabilities. Unlike Nagios, which primarily uses plugins for monitoring, Zabbix offers a more integrated solution with a web-based interface, built-in visualization tools, and advanced features such as automatic discovery and distributed monitoring.

Nagios with Zabbix

While Nagios excels in its simplicity and flexibility with plugins, Zabbix offers a comprehensive, integrated monitoring solution. Using both together can leverage the strengths of each:

- Nagios: Best for quick setup and extensive use of plugins.

- Zabbix: Ideal for detailed performance analysis, real-time data visualization, and advanced features like trend prediction.

Installing and Configuring Zabbix

Install Zabbix Server and Frontend

- Update your package lists and install the Zabbix repository:

```
$ sudo apt update $ sudo apt install wget $ wget
https://repo.zabbix.com/zabbix/6.0/ubuntu/pool/main/z/zab
bix-release/zabbix-release_6.0-1+ubuntu20.04_all.deb $
sudo dpkg -i zabbix-release_6.0-1+ubuntu20.04_all.deb $
sudo apt update
```

- Install the Zabbix server, frontend, and agent:

```
$ sudo apt install zabbix-server-mysql zabbix-frontend-
php zabbix-apache-conf zabbix-agent
```

Configure the Zabbix Database

- Create the initial database and user:

```
$ sudo mysql -uroot -p mysql> create database zabbix
character set utf8mb4 collate utf8mb4_bin; mysql> create
user zabbix@localhost identified by 'yourpassword';
mysql> grant all privileges on zabbix.* to
zabbix@localhost; mysql> quit;
```

- Import the initial schema and data:

```
$ sudo zcat /usr/share/doc/zabbix-server-
mysql*/create.sql.gz | mysql -uzabbix -p zabbix
```

Configure the Zabbix Server

- Edit the Zabbix server configuration file:

```
$ sudo nano /etc/zabbix/zabbix_server.conf
```

- Set the database connection parameters:

```
DBName=zabbix DBUser=zabbix DBPassword=yourpassword
```

Configure PHP for Zabbix Frontend

- Edit the PHP configuration for Zabbix:

```
$ sudo nano /etc/zabbix/apache.conf
```

- Adjust the timezone setting:

```
php_value date.timezone Europe/London
```

- Restart the Apache server:

```
$ sudo systemctl restart apache2
```

- Start the Zabbix server and agent processes:

```
$ sudo systemctl restart zabbix-server zabbix-agent $
sudo systemctl enable zabbix-server zabbix-agent
```

- Open a web browser and navigate to **`http://your_server_ip/zabbix`**. Follow the web-based installation wizard to complete the configuration.

Monitoring Networks and Systems with Nagios and Zabbix

Monitor with Nagios

Using Nagios, set up monitoring for basic services such as HTTP, SSH, and system metrics. Assume these have been configured in previous chapters.

Integrate Zabbix for Advanced Monitoring

Add Zabbix to monitor more detailed metrics and provide comprehensive visualization and analysis.

Configure Zabbix Agent on Monitored Hosts

Install the Zabbix agent on the same or additional hosts:

```
$ sudo apt install zabbix-agent
```

Edit the Zabbix agent configuration file:

```
$ sudo nano /etc/zabbix/zabbix_agentd.conf
```

Set the Zabbix server details:

```
Server=your_zabbix_server_ip
Hostname=your_monitored_host_name
```

Restart the Zabbix agent:

```
$ sudo systemctl restart zabbix-agent $ sudo systemctl
enable zabbix-agent
```

Add Hosts to Zabbix Server

In the Zabbix frontend, go to Configuration > Hosts > Create Host. Fill in the host details, ensuring the host name matches the **`Hostname`** in the agent configuration. Add the appropriate groups and templates for monitoring.

Set Up Triggers and Actions

Define triggers in Zabbix to alert on specific conditions, such as high CPU usage or low disk space. Configure actions to notify administrators via email or other methods.

Trigger for Monitoring CPU Usage with Zabbix can be done as follows:

- Create a Trigger: Go to Configuration > Hosts > [Your Host] > Triggers > Create Trigger.
- Trigger Name: High CPU Usage
- Expression: **{Template OS Linux:system.cpu.util[,idle].avg(5m)}<20**
- Severity: High

This trigger will fire if the average CPU idle time is less than 20% over 5 minutes.

Trigger for Monitoring Disk Space with Zabbix can be done as follows:

    - Create a Trigger: Go to Configuration > Hosts > [Your Host] > Triggers > Create Trigger.
    - Trigger Name: Low Free Disk Space
    - Expression: **{Template OS Linux:vfs.fs.size[/,free].last()}<20G**
    - Severity: High

This trigger will fire if the free disk space on the root filesystem is less than 20GB.

Visualize Data with Zabbix

Use Zabbix's built-in graphing and dashboard capabilities to visualize data from both Nagios and Zabbix agents.

So, lets say, creating a Graph in Zabbix is done as follows:

- Go to Monitoring > Graphs > Create Graph.
- Graph Name: CPU and Memory Usage
- Items: Add items for CPU and memory usage from the monitored host.

This will provide a visual representation of CPU and memory usage over time, helping administrators quickly identify trends and potential issues.

The administrators of AlphaProject can keep a close eye on the system and network performance by using both Nagios for simple monitoring and Zabbix for more in-depth performance analysis. This combined method offers a strong monitoring solution by utilizing the best features of both instruments.

Setting up Alerts and Notifications

To make sure that system administrators are notified quickly of any problems or unusual occurrences, it is crucial to set up alerts and notifications. In this way, issues can be addressed quickly, keeping system performance high and downtime to a minimum. We will set up notifications and alerts for AlphaProject using Zabbix and Nagios, and configure triggers.

Configuring Triggers in Nagios

Triggers in Nagios are defined using service checks that return critical, warning, or OK statuses. These checks are configured to monitor various parameters like disk space, CPU load, memory usage, and more.

Define a Service Check

Edit the Nagios configuration file to define a service check. For example, to check disk space:

```
$ sudo nano
/usr/local/nagios/etc/objects/alphaproject.cfg
```

Add the following service definition:

```
define service { use generic-service host_name
alphaproject_server service_description Disk Space
check_command check_disk!20%!10%!/ }
```

- check_command: Specifies the command to run, in this case, **check_disk**, with warning and critical thresholds of 20% and 10% respectively.

Define Notification Options

Define who gets notified and how. This can be set in the contacts file:

```
$ sudo nano /usr/local/nagios/etc/objects/contacts.cfg
```

Add a contact definition:

```
define contact { contact_name admin alias Admin email
admin@gitforgits.com service_notification_period 24x7
service_notification_options w,u,c,r
service_notification_commands notify-service-by-email }
```

Configure Notification Commands

Edit the commands configuration file to define how notifications are sent:

```
$ sudo nano /usr/local/nagios/etc/objects/commands.cfg
```

Add the notification command:

```
define command { command_name notify-service-by-email
command_line /usr/bin/printf "%b" "***** Nagios
*****\n\nNotification Type:
$NOTIFICATIONTYPE$\n\nService: $SERVICEDESC$\nHost:
$HOSTNAME$\nAddress: $HOSTADDRESS$\nState:
$SERVICESTATE$\n\nDate/Time: $LONGDATETIME$\n\nAdditional
Info:\n\n$SERVICEOUTPUT$\n" | /usr/bin/mail -s "Nagios
Service Alert: $HOSTNAME$/$SERVICEDESC$ is
$SERVICESTATE$" $CONTACTEMAIL$ }
```

Restart Nagios

Apply the configuration changes by restarting Nagios:

```
$ sudo systemctl restart nagios
```

Configuring Triggers in Zabbix

Zabbix provides more advanced trigger configuration options, allowing for complex expressions and conditions.

Create a Trigger

Log in to the Zabbix frontend and navigate to Configuration > Hosts > [Your Host] > Triggers > Create Trigger.

Define the trigger details:

- Name: High CPU Usage
- Expression: **{Template OS Linux:system.cpu.util[,idle].avg(5m)}<20**
- Severity: High

Configure Actions for Notifications

Navigate to Configuration > Actions > Create Action. Define the action details:

- Name: High CPU Usage Notification
- Event Source: Triggers
- Conditions: Trigger severity = High
- Operations: Send message to User Group **Admin**

Define Media Types

Go to Administration > Media Types. Define the email server settings for notifications.

- Name: Email
- Type: Email
- SMTP server: **smtp.gitforgits.com**
- SMTP helo: **gitforgits.com**
- SMTP email: **zabbix@gitforgits.com**

Assign Media to Users

Navigate to Administration > Users > [Admin] > Media > Add. Add the email media type with the email address to receive notifications.

Let us consider creating a trigger and notification for High Memory Usage.

- Create a Trigger for Memory Usage:
    - Name: High Memory Usage
    - Expression: **{Template OS Linux:vm.memory.size[available].last()}<512M**
    - Severity: High
- Create an Action for Memory Usage:
    - Name: High Memory Usage Notification
    - Conditions: Trigger severity = High
    - Operations: Send message to User Group **Admin**
- Configure Media Type:
    - Name: Email
    - SMTP server: **smtp.gitforgits.com**
    - SMTP helo: **gitforgits.com**
    - SMTP email: **zabbix@gitforgits.com**
- Assign Media to Users:
    - Email: **admin@gitforgits.com**

Testing Notifications

To ensure that notifications are working correctly, you can trigger an alert manually:

- Simulate High CPU Usage:
    - On the monitored host, run a CPU-intensive process to simulate high CPU usage.
    - Use **stress** to generate CPU load:

```
$ sudo apt-get install stress $ stress --cpu 4 --timeout
60
```

- Check Zabbix:
    - Verify that the trigger for high CPU usage is activated.
    - Ensure that the email notification is sent to the configured email address.
- Simulate High Memory Usage:
    - On the monitored host, use **stress** to consume memory:

```
$ stress --vm 2 --vm-bytes 1G --timeout 60
```

- Check Notifications:
    - Ensure that the trigger for high memory usage is activated.
    - Verify that the email notification is received.

By combining the two monitoring systems, this setup ensures that the system is always running at its best by providing thorough coverage and timely alerts.

Analyzing System Logs

Overview

System logs contain valuable information about the system's operation, including error messages, security events, and performance metrics. By analyzing these logs, administrators can identify and troubleshoot issues, monitor system performance, ensure security compliance, and maintain overall system health.

Following are the common but key insights from System Logs:

- Error Detection: Logs can reveal errors in applications, services, and system processes, helping to diagnose and fix issues.
- Security Monitoring: Logs can track unauthorized access attempts, policy violations, and other security-related events.
- Performance Monitoring: Logs provide information on resource usage, system performance, and potential bottlenecks.
- Audit and Compliance: Logs can be used to audit system activities and ensure compliance with organizational policies and regulations.

Sample Program: Analyzing System Logs using Nagios and Zabbix

In this section, we will use previously installed Nagios and Zabbix to analyze system logs. We will focus on identifying critical events and monitoring system performance through log analysis.

Using Nagios for Log Analysis

Nagios can be configured to monitor log files and alert administrators to specific events. At first, edit the Nagios configuration to include a new command for log file monitoring.

```
$ sudo nano /usr/local/nagios/etc/objects/commands.cfg
```

Add the following command definition to monitor log files:

```
define command { command_name check_log command_line
/usr/local/nagios/libexec/check_logfiles -f
/path/to/logfile -p /pattern/to/match }
```

Edit the Nagios service configuration file to define a service that uses the **check_log** command.

```
$ sudo nano
/usr/local/nagios/etc/objects/alphaproject.cfg
```

Add the following service definition:

```
define service { use generic-service host_name
alphaproject_server service_description Log File
Monitoring check_command check_log!syslog!/error/ }
```

Apply the configuration changes by restarting Nagios:

```
$ sudo systemctl restart nagios
```

Nagios will now monitor the specified log file for the defined pattern (e.g., "error") and alert administrators if the pattern is found.

Using Zabbix for Log Analysis

Zabbix provides advanced log monitoring capabilities with triggers and alerts based on log file contents. Begin with editing the Zabbix agent configuration file to include log file monitoring.

```
$ sudo nano /etc/zabbix/zabbix_agentd.conf
```

Add the following log monitoring parameters:

```
LogFile=/var/log/syslog LogFileSize=10 Timeout=30 # Log
file monitoring item UserParameter=log.error[*],grep -i
"$1" /var/log/syslog
```

Restart the Zabbix agent to apply changes:

```
$ sudo systemctl restart zabbix-agent
```

Log in to the Zabbix frontend and navigate to Configuration > Hosts > [Your Host] > Items > Create Item.

Define the item details:

- Name: Error Log Monitoring
- Key: log.error[error]
- Type: Zabbix agent
- Type of Information: Log
- Update Interval: 1m

Create a Trigger for Log Monitoring by navigating to Configuration > Hosts > [Your Host] > Triggers > Create Trigger.

Define the trigger details:

- Name: Error Found in Log
- Expression: **{Your_Host:log.error[error].strlen()}>0**
- Severity: High

This trigger will activate if any line in the syslog file contains the word "error".

Then, configure actions for notifications by navigating to Configuration > Actions > Create Action.

Define the action details:

- Name: Log Error Notification
- Event Source: Triggers
- Conditions: Trigger severity = High
- Operations: Send message to User Group **Admin**

For Example: Analyzing Syslog for Errors

1. Generate Log Entries:

- To simulate log entries, add error messages to the syslog:

```
$ logger -p user.err "Test error message for monitoring"
```

2. Check Nagios Alerts:
    - Verify that Nagios detects the error message in the syslog and sends an alert.
3. Check Zabbix Alerts:
    - Verify that Zabbix detects the error message in the syslog and sends a notification.

Using Logwatch for Detailed Log Analysis

Logwatch is another tool that provides detailed analysis of log files and generates reports.

```
$ sudo apt-get install logwatch
```

Generate a report for the syslog:

```
$ sudo logwatch --detail high --logfile syslog --range
today --service all --print
```

Following is the desired output:

```
-------------------- Logwatch 7.5.2 (03/22/20) -----------
--------- Processing Initiated: Fri Apr 15 13:45:19 2022
Date Range Processed: today ( 2022-Apr-15 ) Period is
day. Detail Level of Output: 10 Type of Output/Format:
stdout / text Logfiles for Host: AlphaProject -----------
-----------------------------------------------------
################### Log Summary ###################
/var/log/syslog: ------------------------ 1 error: - Test
error message for monitoring ---------------------------
--------------------- ################ End of Logwatch
Log Summary #####################
```

This output summarizes log entries, highlighting errors and other significant events.

By using Nagios, Zabbix, and Logwatch, system administrators can effectively analyze system logs, identify critical events, and ensure the overall health and security of AlphaProject. Regular log analysis helps in maintaining system performance, troubleshooting issues, and ensuring compliance with security policies.

Performance Tuning

Overview

The system's efficiency and its ability to handle workloads effectively are guaranteed through performance tuning. Here, we will go over the possible optimizations for AlphaProject and show you how to tune its performance using the tools you already have.

Recap of Performance Aspects:

- Monitoring and optimizing CPU usage to prevent bottlenecks.
- Managing memory usage to avoid swapping and ensure efficient resource utilization.
- Reducing disk I/O operations to improve read/write performance.
- Ensuring network efficiency to handle data transmission effectively.
- Optimizing database queries and configurations for faster response times.

Step-by-Step Performance Tuning

To explore practical performance tuning, we will use tools such as **`top`**, **`htop`**, **`vmstat`**, and **`iostat`** for performance monitoring and tuning, and **`sysctl`** for tuning kernel parameters.

Monitoring CPU Usage

Use **`top`** and **`htop`** to identify processes consuming high CPU resources.

```
$ top
```

Look for processes with high **`%CPU`**. If a process is consistently using a high amount of CPU, consider optimizing or distributing its workload.

```
$ htop
```

Use the interactive interface to sort processes by CPU usage and identify the resource-intensive ones.

Optimizing Memory Usage

Monitor memory usage using **`vmstat`** to identify memory bottlenecks.

```
$ vmstat 5
```

Following is the desired output:

```
procs -----------memory---------- ---swap-- -----io---- -
system-- ------cpu----- r b swpd free buff cache si so bi
bo in cs us sy id wa st 2 0 10240 204800 50000 102400 0 0
1 2 10 20 5 2 90 3 0
```

Focus on **si** (swap in) and **so** (swap out) columns. High values indicate heavy swapping, suggesting the need for more RAM or better memory management.

Reducing Disk I/O

Use **iostat** to monitor disk I/O performance.

```
$ iostat -dx 5
```

Following is the desired output:

```
Device: rrqm/s wrqm/s r/s w/s rMB/s wMB/s avgrq-sz avgqu-
sz await r_await w_await svctm %util sda 0.00 0.00 0.40
1.20 0.01 0.05 72.00 0.10 8.00 8.00 8.00 1.50 0.20
```

Wherein,

- r/s and w/s: Read and write requests per second.
- await: Average wait time for I/O operations.
- %util: Percentage of time the device is active.

High values in **await** or **%util** indicate disk I/O bottlenecks. Consider using faster storage solutions or optimizing disk usage patterns.

Enhancing Network Performance

Use **iftop** to monitor network traffic and identify bandwidth issues.

```
$ sudo iftop -i eth0
```

Identify hosts consuming excessive bandwidth and examine further. Consider optimizing network configurations or upgrading network hardware if necessary.

Database Performance Tuning

Optimize database performance using **pg_stat_statements** in PostgreSQL.

- Enable pg_stat_statements:

```
$ sudo -u postgres psql postgres=# CREATE EXTENSION
pg_stat_statements;
```

- Analyze Queries:

```
postgres=# SELECT * FROM pg_stat_statements ORDER BY
total_time DESC LIMIT 5;
```

- Identify slow queries and optimize them by creating indexes, rewriting queries, or adjusting database configurations.

Kernel Parameter Tuning

Let us consider an example to increase TCP Buffer Sizes wherein, you use **sysctl** to adjust kernel parameters for better performance.

```
$ sudo sysctl -w net.core.rmem_max=16777216 $ sudo sysctl
-w net.core.wmem_max=16777216 $ sudo sysctl -w
net.ipv4.tcp_rmem="4096 87380 16777216" $ sudo sysctl -w
net.ipv4.tcp_wmem="4096 65536 16777216"
```

Make the changes permanent by editing **/etc/sysctl.conf**:

```
$ sudo nano /etc/sysctl.conf
```

Add the following lines:

```
net.core.rmem_max=16777216 net.core.wmem_max=16777216
net.ipv4.tcp_rmem=4096 87380 16777216
net.ipv4.tcp_wmem=4096 65536 16777216
```

You can make sure that AlphaProject runs well and can manage increasing workloads by carefully watching and adjusting every part of the system. If you want your system to run at peak efficiency and avoid any slowdowns, you need to tune these performance indicators regularly.

Maintaining System Uptime

Overview

Maintaining system uptime is crucial for ensuring that services remain available and operational, even in the face of failures or challenges.

Key Scenarios for Maintaining Uptime

- Hardware Failures
- Software Crashes
- Network Issues
- Power Outages
- Planned Maintenance

Tools and Techniques

- High Availability (HA) Clustering
- Load Balancing
- Redundant Systems
- Automated Failover
- Monitoring and Alerting

High Availability Clustering

High Availability (HA) clustering ensures that if one node fails, another can take over its workload.

Install and Configure HA Cluster

Use tools like Pacemaker and Corosync to set up an HA cluster.

```
$ sudo apt-get install pacemaker corosync
```

Edit the Corosync configuration file:

```
$ sudo nano /etc/corosync/corosync.conf
```

Following is the sample configuration:

```
totem { version: 2 secauth: on threads: 0 interface {
ringnumber: 0 bindnetaddr: 192.168.1.0 mcastaddr:
239.255.1.1 mcastport: 5405 } } quorum { provider:
corosync_votequorum two_node: 1 }
```

Start and enable the services:

```
$ sudo systemctl start corosync $ sudo systemctl start
pacemaker $ sudo systemctl enable corosync $ sudo
systemctl enable pacemaker
```

Add nodes to the cluster:

```
$ sudo pcs cluster auth node1 node2 $ sudo pcs cluster
setup --name mycluster node1 node2 $ sudo pcs cluster
start --all
```

Create Resources and Constraints

Create resources for the services you want to maintain high availability for, such as a web server.

```
$ sudo pcs resource create WebServer ocf:heartbeat:apache
configfile=/etc/apache2/apache2.conf op monitor
interval=30s
```

Set constraints to ensure the resource runs on only one node at a time:

```
$ sudo pcs constraint colocation add WebServer with
WebServer-clone INFINITY $ sudo pcs constraint order
WebServer then WebServer-clone
```

Load Balancing

Load balancing distributes incoming network traffic across multiple servers to ensure no single server becomes overwhelmed.

- Install HAProxy:

```
$ sudo apt-get install haproxy
```

- Configure HAProxy to balance traffic between backend servers:

```
$ sudo nano /etc/haproxy/haproxy.cfg
```

Following is the sample configuration:

```
frontend http_front bind *:80 stats uri /haproxy?stats
default_backend http_back backend http_back balance
roundrobin server server1 192.168.1.101:80 check server
server2 192.168.1.102:80 check
```

- Restart HAProxy:

```
$ sudo systemctl restart haproxy
```

Redundant Systems

Implementing redundant systems ensures that if one component fails, another can take over without service interruption.

Set up Redundant Servers

Ensure critical services are running on multiple servers. For example, to replicate a database across multiple nodes, edit the MySQL configuration on the master server:

```
$ sudo nano /etc/mysql/mysql.conf.d/mysqld.cnf
```

Add the following lines:

```
[mysqld] log_bin = /var/log/mysql/mysql-bin.log server_id
= 1 binlog_do_db = mydatabase
```

Restart MySQL:

```
$ sudo systemctl restart mysql
```

On the slave server, edit the MySQL configuration:

```
$ sudo nano /etc/mysql/mysql.conf.d/mysqld.cnf
```

Add the following lines:

```
[mysqld] server_id = 2
```

Restart MySQL:

```
$ sudo systemctl restart mysql
```

Configure Replication

On the master server, create a replication user:

```
mysql> CREATE USER 'replicator'@'%' IDENTIFIED BY
'password'; mysql> GRANT REPLICATION SLAVE ON *.* TO
'replicator'@'%';
```

On the slave server, set up replication:

```
mysql> CHANGE MASTER TO MASTER_HOST='master_ip',
MASTER_USER='replicator', MASTER_PASSWORD='password',
MASTER_LOG_FILE='mysql-bin.000001', MASTER_LOG_POS=0;
mysql> START SLAVE;
```

Check the replication status:

```
mysql> SHOW SLAVE STATUS\G
```

Automated Failover

Automated failover ensures that if a primary system fails, a backup system can take over automatically. To begin with, first install Keepalived as repeated in one of thee previous chapter:

```
$ sudo apt-get install keepalived
```

Configure Keepalived on both the primary and backup servers:

```
$ sudo nano /etc/keepalived/keepalived.conf
```

Following is the sample configuration for the primary server:

```
vrrp_script chk_haproxy { script "killall -0 haproxy"
interval 2 } vrrp_instance VI_1 { interface eth0 state
MASTER virtual_router_id 51 priority 100 advert_int 1
authentication { auth_type PASS auth_pass 1234 }
virtual_ipaddress { 192.168.1.100 } track_script {
chk_haproxy } }
```

Following is the sample configuration for the backup server:

```
vrrp_script chk_haproxy { script "killall -0 haproxy"
interval 2 } vrrp_instance VI_1 { interface eth0 state
BACKUP virtual_router_id 51 priority 90 advert_int 1
authentication { auth_type PASS auth_pass 1234 }
virtual_ipaddress { 192.168.1.100 } track_script {
chk_haproxy } }
```

Restart Keepalived:

```
$ sudo systemctl restart keepalived
```

Monitoring and Alerting

Use tools like Nagios and Zabbix to monitor system health and set up alerts for any issues that could impact uptime.

Configure Nagios and Zabbix for Monitoring

Ensure both Nagios and Zabbix are configured to monitor key system metrics such as CPU, memory, disk space, and network performance, as learned in previous sections.

Set up Alerts

Configure alerts to notify administrators of any critical issues. For example, set up email alerts in Nagios for high CPU usage:

```
$ sudo nano /usr/local/nagios/etc/objects/commands.cfg
```

Add the notification command:

```
define command { command_name notify-service-by-email
command_line /usr/bin/printf "%b" "***** Nagios
*****\n\nNotification Type:
$NOTIFICATIONTYPE$\n\nService: $SERVICEDESC$\nHost:
$HOSTNAME$\nAddress: $HOSTADDRESS$\nState:
$SERVICESTATE$\n\nDate/Time: $LONGDATETIME$\n\nAdditional
Info:\n\n$SERVICEOUTPUT$\n" | /usr/bin/mail -s "Nagios
Service Alert: $HOSTNAME$/$SERVICEDESC$ is
$SERVICESTATE$" $CONTACTEMAIL$ }
```

By utilizing these strategies and tools, you can effectively maintain AlphaProject's system uptime, making sure that services remain available and operational even in the face of failure scenarios.

Summary

Just to sum up, the focus of this chapter was on system health monitoring, encompassing various essential techniques and tools to ensure optimal system performance and reliability. It began with monitoring CPU and memory usage, highlighting the importance of tracking these resources to prevent bottlenecks. Tools like **top**, **htop**, and **vmstat** were utilized to monitor and analyze system performance metrics. Disk space monitoring and management were addressed next, using commands such as **df**, **du**, and **iostat** to assess disk usage and identify potential issues. Tracking network performance involved commands like **ping**, **traceroute**, **iftop**, and **vnstat**, providing insights into network traffic and connectivity.

The chapter also covered the use of **top** and **htop** for real-time system monitoring, allowing administrators to identify resource-intensive processes and manage them effectively. Monitoring with Nagios and Zabbix was explored, demonstrating how these tools complement each other in providing comprehensive monitoring solutions. Triggers, alerts, and notifications were configured to ensure timely responses to system issues. Analyzing system logs was highlighted as a crucial aspect of monitoring, using tools like Nagios, Zabbix, and Logwatch to extract valuable information from logs for troubleshooting and security monitoring.

Performance tuning was learned, focusing on optimizing CPU, memory, disk I/O, and network performance. Tools like **`sysctl`** were used for tuning kernel parameters. Finally, maintaining system uptime was addressed, covering strategies such as high availability clustering, load balancing, redundant systems, automated failover, and robust monitoring and alerting systems. These techniques aimed to ensure that services remained operational even in the face of hardware failures, software crashes, network issues, power outages, and planned maintenance. This comprehensive approach to system health monitoring equipped you and practicing system administrators with the skills and knowledge to maintain a stable and efficient computing environment.

CHAPTER 6: AUTOMATION AND SCRIPTING

Introduction

Shell scripting is a powerful tool for system administrators, and this chapter will introduce you to it. Shell scripting is introduced in this chapter with an introduction that covers the basics and how important it is for automating routine tasks. Using variables and control structures, you will learn to develop basic scripts that can handle diverse system operations efficiently and dynamically.

Moving on to the next topic, "automating system tasks," this chapter delves into the ins and outs of cron and anacron script scheduling and management, allowing users to set up automatic job execution at predetermined times. We will learn about how to use awk and sed to process text and show how these tools can make it easier to change and analyze text files.

Also covered is how to create scripts for system audits, so you can keep an eye on your system's security and health and report back to your boss as necessary. We will go over ways to automate resource management and show you how to write scripts that efficiently handle things like memory, storage space, and CPU. At last, the chapter will go over the process of making backup and recovery scripts, which will make sure that important data is backed up automatically and can be readily recovered in the event that data loss occurs.

Shell Scripting Overview

There are a lot of benefits to shell scripting, and it helps system administrators manage and automate activities much more efficiently. Automation is the main advantage of shell scripting. It helps system administrators to reduce human error and manual intervention by automating repetitive processes. System administration becomes more consistent and productive as a result. Shell scripting also makes it easier to run complicated command sequences that would be tedious to run by hand.

Advantages of Shell Scripting

- Automate routine tasks like backups, system updates, and user management.
- Execute multiple commands in sequence without manual intervention, saving time and effort.
- Ensure that tasks are performed the same way every time, reducing the chance of errors.
- Handle complex tasks that involve multiple steps and dependencies.
- Tailor scripts to meet specific administrative needs and workflows.
- Easily scale operations across multiple systems by deploying scripts across servers.

Automation Scripting Use-Cases

Backup and Recovery

Shell scripting can automate the backup of critical data, reducing the risk of data loss and ensuring that backups are performed consistently. A script can be scheduled to run at regular intervals, creating backups and storing them securely.

Following is the sample script:

```
#!/bin/bash BACKUP_DIR="/backup" SOURCE_DIR="/data"
TIMESTAMP=$(date +%F) BACKUP_FILE="$BACKUP_DIR/backup-
$TIMESTAMP.tar.gz" tar -czf $BACKUP_FILE $SOURCE_DIR echo
"Backup created at $BACKUP_FILE"
```

This script compresses the contents of the **/data** directory into a tarball and stores it in the **/backup** directory with a timestamp.

System Updates

Keeping the system and software up-to-date is crucial for security and performance. Shell scripts can automate the update process, ensuring that updates are applied regularly without manual intervention.

Following is the sample script:

```
#!/bin/bash apt-get update apt-get upgrade -y echo
"System updated on $(date)"
```

This script updates the package list and upgrades all installed packages, logging the update time.

User Management

Managing user accounts can be automated to streamline the process of adding, modifying, and removing users. This is particularly useful in environments with high user turnover or where user settings need to be standardized.

Following is the sample script:

```
#!/bin/bash USERNAME=$1 PASSWORD=$2 if id "$USERNAME"
&>/dev/null; then echo "User $USERNAME already exists"
else useradd -m $USERNAME echo "$USERNAME:$PASSWORD" |
chpasswd echo "User $USERNAME created" fi
```

This script creates a new user with a specified username and password if the user does not already exist.

Resource Monitoring

Regularly monitoring system resources helps prevent issues before they become critical. Scripts can be used to check resource usage and send alerts if usage exceeds certain thresholds.

Following is the sample script:

```
#!/bin/bash THRESHOLD=80 USAGE=$(df / | grep / | awk
'{print $5}' | sed 's/%//') if [ $USAGE -gt $THRESHOLD ];
then echo "Disk usage is above $THRESHOLD% on
$(hostname)" | mail -s "Disk Usage Alert"
admin@gitforgits.com fi
```

This script checks the disk usage of the root filesystem and sends an email alert if usage exceeds 80%.

Log Management

Logs are essential for diagnosing issues and auditing system activities. Automating log management ensures that logs are rotated, compressed, and archived, freeing up disk space and keeping the system organized.

Following is the sample script:

```
#!/bin/bash LOG_DIR="/var/log/myapp"
ARCHIVE_DIR="/var/log/archive" find $LOG_DIR -type f -
mtime +30 -exec gzip {} \; find $LOG_DIR -type f -name
"*.gz" -exec mv {} $ARCHIVE_DIR \;
```

This script compresses log files older than 30 days and moves them to an archive directory.

Task Scheduling

Shell scripts can be scheduled using cron to perform regular maintenance tasks, ensuring the system remains in optimal condition without requiring manual intervention.

Following is the sample script of Cron Job:

```
0 2 * * * /path/to/backup.sh
```

This cron job schedules the backup script to run daily at 2 AM.

Sample Program: Automating Daily Report Generation

A common task for system administrators is generating daily reports on system health and performance. This can be automated using shell scripting.

Following is the sample daily report script:

```
#!/bin/bash REPORT_FILE="/var/reports/daily-report-$(date
+%F).txt" echo "System Report for $(date)" > $REPORT_FILE
echo "" >> $REPORT_FILE echo "Disk Usage:" >>
$REPORT_FILE df -h >> $REPORT_FILE echo "" >>
$REPORT_FILE echo "Memory Usage:" >> $REPORT_FILE free -m
>> $REPORT_FILE echo "" >> $REPORT_FILE echo "Top
Processes:" >> $REPORT_FILE top -b -n 1 | head -n 20 >>
$REPORT_FILE echo "" >> $REPORT_FILE echo "Network
Usage:" >> $REPORT_FILE vnstat -d >> $REPORT_FILE echo ""
>> $REPORT_FILE echo "Report generated and saved to
$REPORT_FILE"
```

This script generates a comprehensive report on disk usage, memory usage, top processes, and network usage, and saves it to a file with a timestamp.

Writing Basic Automation Scripts

Writing basic scripts is the first step toward automating tasks in a Linux environment. In this section, we will cover writing simple automation scripts for the AlphaProject, including multiple scenarios to demonstrate different aspects of shell scripting.

Scenario 1: Automating a Directory Backup

A common task is backing up a directory to ensure data is safe. We will create a script to automate this process for the AlphaProject.

Following is the directory backup script:

```
#!/bin/bash # Backup script for AlphaProject
SOURCE_DIR="/var/www/alphaproject"
BACKUP_DIR="/backup/alphaproject" TIMESTAMP=$(date
+%Y%m%d%H%M%S) BACKUP_FILE="$BACKUP_DIR/backup-
$TIMESTAMP.tar.gz" echo "Starting backup of $SOURCE_DIR
to $BACKUP_FILE" mkdir -p $BACKUP_DIR tar -czf
$BACKUP_FILE $SOURCE_DIR echo "Backup completed
successfully!"
```

In the above code snippet,

1. Variables: Define source and backup directories, and create a timestamp for the backup file name.
2. Commands:
    - **mkdir -p $BACKUP_DIR**: Create the backup directory if it doesn't exist.
    - **tar -czf $BACKUP_FILE $SOURCE_DIR**: Compress the source directory into a tar.gz file.

Running the script:

```
$ chmod +x backup.sh $ ./backup.sh
```

Following is the output:

```
Starting backup of /var/www/alphaproject to
/backup/alphaproject/backup-20240520.tar.gz Backup
completed successfully!
```

Scenario 2: System Update Automation

Updating the system regularly is crucial. We will create a script to automate system updates.

Following is the system update script:

```
#!/bin/bash # System update script echo "Updating system
packages" sudo apt-get update sudo apt-get upgrade -y
echo "System update completed successfully!"
```

In the above code snippet,

- **sudo apt-get update**: Update the package list.
- **sudo apt-get upgrade -y**: Upgrade all installed packages automatically.

Running the script:

```
$ chmod +x update.sh $ ./update.sh
```

Following is the output:

```
Updating system packages ... System update completed
successfully!
```

Scenario 3: Disk Usage Monitoring

Monitoring disk usage helps prevent storage issues. We will create a script to check disk usage and alert if it exceeds a threshold.

Following is the disk usage script:

```
#!/bin/bash # Disk usage monitoring script THRESHOLD=80
USAGE=$(df / | grep / | awk '{print $5}' | sed 's/%//')
if [ $USAGE -gt $THRESHOLD ]; then echo "Disk usage is
above $THRESHOLD% on $(hostname)" | mail -s "Disk Usage
Alert" admin@gitforgits.com fi
```

In the above code snippet,

- Variables: Define the usage threshold.
- Commands:
  - **df /**: Check disk usage of the root filesystem.
  - **grep /**: Filter the output for the root filesystem.
  - **awk '{print $5}'**: Extract the usage percentage.
  - **sed 's/%//'**: Remove the percentage sign.

Running the script:

```
$ chmod +x disk_usage.sh $ ./disk_usage.sh
```

Following is the output (if threshold exceeded):

```
Disk usage is above 80% on alphaproject-server
```

Scenario 4: User Account Management

Managing user accounts can be automated. We will create a script to add a new user and set a password.

Following is the user management script:

```
#!/bin/bash # User management script USERNAME=$1
PASSWORD=$2 if id "$USERNAME" &>/dev/null; then echo
"User $USERNAME already exists" else sudo useradd -m
$USERNAME echo "$USERNAME:$PASSWORD" | sudo chpasswd echo
"User $USERNAME created and password set" fi
```

In the above code snippet,

- Variables: Accept username and password as arguments.
- Commands:
    - **id "$USERNAME"**: Check if the user exists.
    - **sudo useradd -m $USERNAME**: Create the user if they don't exist.
    - **echo "$USERNAME:$PASSWORD" | sudo chpasswd**: Set the user's password.

Running the script:

```
$ chmod +x user_management.sh $ ./user_management.sh
newuser newpassword
```

Following is the output:

```
User newuser created and password set
```

Scenario 5: Log File Cleanup

Automating log file cleanup helps manage disk space. We will create a script to clean up old log files.

Following is the log cleanup script:

```
#!/bin/bash # Log cleanup script
LOG_DIR="/var/log/alphaproject" DAYS=30 echo "Cleaning up
log files older than $DAYS days in $LOG_DIR" find
$LOG_DIR -type f -mtime +$DAYS -exec rm -f {} \; echo
"Log cleanup completed"
```

In the above code snippet,

- Variables: Define the log directory and the age threshold for logs.
- Commands:
    - **find $LOG_DIR -type f -mtime +$DAYS -exec rm -f {} \;**: Find and delete files older than the specified number of days.

Running the script:

```
$ chmod +x log_cleanup.sh $ ./log_cleanup.sh
```

Following is the output:

```
Cleaning up log files older than 30 days in
/var/log/alphaproject Log cleanup completed
```

Scenario 6: Network Health Check

Automating network health checks ensures connectivity. We will create a script to ping a list of servers and report their status.

Following is the network health check script:

```
#!/bin/bash # Network health check script
SERVERS=("192.168.1.1" "192.168.1.2"
"www.gitforgits.com")
LOGFILE="/var/log/network_health.log" echo "Checking
network health on $(date)" >> $LOGFILE for SERVER in
"${SERVERS[@]}"; do ping -c 1 $SERVER &> /dev/null if [
$? -eq 0 ]; then echo "$SERVER is reachable" >> $LOGFILE
else echo "$SERVER is unreachable" >> $LOGFILE fi done
echo "Network health check completed" >> $LOGFILE
```

In the above code snippet,

- Variables: Define an array of servers to check and a log file.
- Commands:
    - **ping -c 1 $SERVER**: Ping each server once.
    - **if [$? -eq 0]; then**: Check the ping command's exit status.

Running the script:

```
$ chmod +x network_health.sh $ ./network_health.sh
```

Following is the output (in log file):

```
Checking network health on 2024-05-20 192.168.1.1 is
reachable 192.168.1.2 is reachable www.gitforgits.com is
reachable Network health check completed
```

Making use of these simple scripts, system administrators can automate a number of AlphaProject processes, leading to greater efficiency and the reliable execution of mission-critical processes.

Using Variables and Control Structures

Shell programming relies heavily on control structures and variables. With their help, scripts can remember information, respond in response to new circumstances, and make judgments. In this section we will improve the automation scripts learned in the last section by adding variables and control structures. In addition, to make the scripts more versatile and powerful, we will also offer new kinds of variables and control structures.

Types of Variables

1. Local Variables: Defined within a script and not accessible outside it.
2. Environment Variables: Available to the current shell session and any subprocesses.
3. Positional Parameters: Special variables ($0, $1, $2, ...) representing arguments passed to the script.

Control Structures

1. if-else: Executes code based on conditions.
2. for: Iterates over a list of items.
3. while: Repeats a block of code while a condition is true.
4. case: Selects code to execute based on the value of a variable.

Enhancing Automation Scripts

Scenario 1: Automating a Directory Backup with Variables and Control Structures

Following is the enhanced backup script:

```
#!/bin/bash # Enhanced Backup script for AlphaProject
SOURCE_DIR="/var/www/alphaproject"
BACKUP_DIR="/backup/alphaproject" TIMESTAMP=$(date
+%Y%m%d%H%M%S) BACKUP_FILE="$BACKUP_DIR/backup-
$TIMESTAMP.tar.gz" if [ ! -d "$SOURCE_DIR" ]; then echo
"Source directory $SOURCE_DIR does not exist." exit 1 fi
if [ ! -d "$BACKUP_DIR" ]; then mkdir -p $BACKUP_DIR echo
"Backup directory $BACKUP_DIR created." fi echo "Starting
backup of $SOURCE_DIR to $BACKUP_FILE" tar -czf
$BACKUP_FILE $SOURCE_DIR if [ $? -eq 0 ]; then echo
"Backup completed successfully!" else echo "Backup
failed!" exit 1 fi
```

In the above code snippet,

1. Variables: SOURCE_DIR, BACKUP_DIR, TIMESTAMP, BACKUP_FILE.
2. if-else: Check if directories exist and if the backup command succeeds.

Running the script:

```
$ chmod +x enhanced_backup.sh $ ./enhanced_backup.sh
```

Following is the output:

```
Backup directory /backup/alphaproject created. Starting
backup of /var/www/alphaproject to
/backup/alphaproject/backup-20240520.tar.gz Backup
completed successfully!
```

Scenario 2: System Update Automation with Variables and Control Structures

Following is the enhanced system update script:

```
#!/bin/bash # Enhanced System update script
LOGFILE="/var/log/system_update.log" DATE=$(date) echo
"System update started at $DATE" | tee -a $LOGFILE if !
sudo apt-get update; then echo "Failed to update package
list" | tee -a $LOGFILE exit 1 fi if ! sudo apt-get
upgrade -y; then echo "Failed to upgrade packages" | tee
-a $LOGFILE exit 1 fi echo "System update completed
successfully at $(date)" | tee -a $LOGFILE
```

In the above code snippet,

1. Variables: LOGFILE, DATE.
2. if-else: Check if update and upgrade commands succeed.

Running the script:

```
$ chmod +x enhanced_update.sh $ ./enhanced_update.sh
```

Following is the output:

```
System update started at Mon May 20 10:00:00 UTC 2024 ...
System update completed successfully at Mon May 20
10:05:00 UTC 2024
```

Scenario 3: Disk Usage Monitoring with Variables and Control Structures

Following is the enhanced disk usage script:

```
#!/bin/bash # Enhanced Disk usage monitoring script
THRESHOLD=80 LOGFILE="/var/log/disk_usage.log" USAGE=$(df
/ | grep / | awk '{print $5}' | sed 's/%//') echo "Disk
usage check at $(date)" >> $LOGFILE if [ $USAGE -gt
$THRESHOLD ]; then echo "Disk usage is above $THRESHOLD%
on $(hostname)" | tee -a $LOGFILE | mail -s "Disk Usage
Alert" admin@gitforgits.com else echo "Disk usage is
below $THRESHOLD%. Current usage: $USAGE%" >> $LOGFILE fi
```

In the above code snippet,

1. Variables: THRESHOLD, LOGFILE, USAGE.
2. if-else: Check if disk usage exceeds the threshold and log the results.

Running the script:

```
$ chmod +x enhanced_disk_usage.sh $
./enhanced_disk_usage.sh
```

Following is the output (in log file):

```
Disk usage check at Mon May 20 10:10:00 UTC 2024 Disk
usage is below 80%. Current usage: 45%
```

Scenario 4: User Account Management with Variables and Control Structures

Following is the enhanced user management script:

```
#!/bin/bash # Enhanced User management script USERNAME=$1
PASSWORD=$2 LOGFILE="/var/log/user_management.log" if [ -
z "$USERNAME" ] || [ -z "$PASSWORD" ]; then echo "Usage:
$0 USERNAME PASSWORD" | tee -a $LOGFILE exit 1 fi if id
"$USERNAME" &>/dev/null; then echo "User $USERNAME
already exists" | tee -a $LOGFILE else sudo useradd -m
$USERNAME echo "$USERNAME:$PASSWORD" | sudo chpasswd if [
$? -eq 0 ]; then echo "User $USERNAME created and
password set" | tee -a $LOGFILE else echo "Failed to
create user $USERNAME" | tee -a $LOGFILE exit 1 fi fi
```

In the above code snippet,

1. Variables: USERNAME, PASSWORD, LOGFILE.
2. if-else: Check if the username and password are provided, and handle user creation or existence check.

Running the script:

```
$ chmod +x enhanced_user_management.sh $
./enhanced_user_management.sh newuser newpassword
```

Following is the output:

```
User newuser created and password set
```

Scenario 5: Log File Cleanup with Variables and Control Structures

Following is the enhanced log cleanup script:

```
#!/bin/bash # Enhanced Log cleanup script
LOG_DIR="/var/log/alphaproject"
ARCHIVE_DIR="/var/log/archive" DAYS=30
LOGFILE="/var/log/log_cleanup.log" echo "Log cleanup
started at $(date)" >> $LOGFILE if [ ! -d "$ARCHIVE_DIR"
]; then mkdir -p $ARCHIVE_DIR echo "Archive directory
$ARCHIVE_DIR created." >> $LOGFILE fi find $LOG_DIR -type
f -mtime +$DAYS -exec gzip {} \; find $LOG_DIR -type f -
name "*.gz" -exec mv {} $ARCHIVE_DIR \; if [ $? -eq 0 ];
then echo "Log cleanup completed successfully at $(date)"
>> $LOGFILE else echo "Log cleanup failed at $(date)" >>
$LOGFILE fi
```

In the above code snippet,

1. Variables: LOG_DIR, ARCHIVE_DIR, DAYS, LOGFILE.
2. if-else: Check if the archive directory exists and handle the log cleanup process.

Running the script:

```
$ chmod +x enhanced_log_cleanup.sh $
./enhanced_log_cleanup.sh
```

Following is the output (in log file):

```
Log cleanup started at Mon May 20 10:20:00 UTC 2024
Archive directory /var/log/archive created. Log cleanup
completed successfully at Mon May 20 10:21:00 UTC 2024
```

Scenario 6: Network Health Check with Variables and Control Structures

Following is the enhanced network health check script:

```
#!/bin/bash # Enhanced Network health check script
SERVERS=("192.168.1.1" "192.168.1.2"
"www.gitforgits.com")
LOGFILE="/var/log/network_health.log" echo "Checking
network health on $(date)" >> $LOGFILE for SERVER in
"${SERVERS[@]}"; do ping -c 1 $SERVER &> /dev/null if [
$? -eq 0 ]; then echo "$SERVER is reachable" >> $LOGFILE
else echo "$SERVER is unreachable" >> $LOGFILE fi done
echo "Network health check completed" >> $LOGFILE
```

In the above code snippet,

1. Variables: SERVERS (array), LOGFILE.
2. for loop: Iterate over the list of servers.
3. if-else: Check the result of the ping command for each server.

Running the script:

```
$ chmod +x enhanced_network_health.sh $
./enhanced_network_health.sh
```

Following is the output (in log file):

```
Checking network health on Mon May 20 10:30:00 UTC 2024
192.168.1.1 is reachable 192.168.1.2 is reachable
www.gitforgits.com is reachable Network health check
completed
```

Adding variables and control structures to our AlphaProject scripts has made them more functional and flexible. The scripts are now more capable of handling different conditions and automating chores more effectively thanks to these modifications.

Managing Task Automation with 'cron' and 'anacron'

Introduction to 'anacron'

In system administration, scheduling tasks to run automatically at specified intervals is essential for maintaining system performance and consistency. While **cron** is used for scheduling tasks that need to run at precise times or intervals, **anacron** is useful for running tasks that need to be executed periodically, but not necessarily at specific times. **anacron** is a task scheduler that is designed for systems that are not always running. Unlike **cron**, which requires the system to be up at the time the task is scheduled, **anacron** ensures that periodic tasks are run even if the system was down at the scheduled time. It is ideal for laptops, desktops, or any systems that do not run continuously. The anacron configuration files are typically located in **/etc/anacrontab**.

Writing Automation Scripts with 'cron'

To edit the crontab file for scheduling tasks:

```
$ crontab -e
```

- Hourly Task:

```
0 * * * * /path/to/hourly_task.sh
```

This entry schedules the **hourly_task.sh** script to run at the beginning of every hour.

- Weekly Task:

```
0 2 * * 0 /path/to/weekly_task.sh
```

This entry schedules the **weekly_task.sh** script to run every Sunday at 2 AM.

- Yearly Task:

```
0 0 1 1 * /path/to/yearly_task.sh
```

This entry schedules the **yearly_task.sh** script to run at midnight on January 1st every year.

Following is the sample script:

```
#!/bin/bash # hourly_task.sh echo "Hourly task executed
at $(date)" >> /var/log/hourly_task.log
```

Sometimes tasks need to run asynchronously without blocking other operations. This can be achieved using **&** to run tasks in the background.

```
#!/bin/bash # async_task.sh (sleep 30; echo "Async task
completed at $(date)" >> /var/log/async_task.log) &
```

Writing Automation Scripts with 'anacron'

Edit the **/etc/anacrontab** file to schedule tasks:

```
$ sudo nano /etc/anacrontab
```

Example Entries:

- Daily Task:

```
1 5 cron.daily run-parts /etc/cron.daily
```

This entry schedules all scripts in **/etc/cron.daily** to run 5 minutes after **anacron** starts if they haven't been run in the last day.

- Weekly Task:

```
7 10 cron.weekly run-parts /etc/cron.weekly
```

This entry schedules all scripts in **/etc/cron.weekly** to run 10 minutes after **anacron** starts if they haven't been run in the last week.

- Monthly Task:

```
@monthly 15 cron.monthly run-parts /etc/cron.monthly
```

This entry schedules all scripts in **/etc/cron.monthly** to run 15 minutes after **anacron** starts if they haven't been run in the last month.

Following is the sample script:

```
#!/bin/bash # daily_task.sh echo "Daily task executed at
$(date)" >> /var/log/daily_task.log
```

Place this script in **/etc/cron.daily** to have it executed by **anacron**.

Example 1: Hourly Backup Script (cron)

```
#!/bin/bash # hourly_backup.sh
SOURCE_DIR="/var/www/alphaproject"
BACKUP_DIR="/backup/alphaproject" TIMESTAMP=$(date
+%Y%m%d%H) BACKUP_FILE="$BACKUP_DIR/backup-
$TIMESTAMP.tar.gz" tar -czf $BACKUP_FILE $SOURCE_DIR echo
"Hourly backup created at $BACKUP_FILE"
```

Crontab Entry:

```
0 * * * * /path/to/hourly_backup.sh
```

Example 2: Weekly Maintenance Script (anacron)

```
#!/bin/bash # weekly_maintenance.sh echo "Weekly
maintenance started at $(date)" >>
/var/log/maintenance.log apt-get update && apt-get
upgrade -y echo "Weekly maintenance completed at $(date)"
>> /var/log/maintenance.log
```

anacrontab Entry:

```
7 10 cron.weekly run-parts /etc/cron.weekly
```

Place the script in **/etc/cron.weekly**.

Example 3: Yearly Audit Script (cron)

```
#!/bin/bash # yearly_audit.sh echo "Yearly audit started
at $(date)" >> /var/log/audit.log # Audit commands echo
"Yearly audit completed at $(date)" >> /var/log/audit.log
```

Crontab Entry:

```
0 0 1 1 * /path/to/yearly_audit.sh
```

Example 4: Asynchronous Cleanup Script (cron)

```
#!/bin/bash # async_cleanup.sh (sleep 120; echo "Cleanup
task completed at $(date)" >> /var/log/cleanup.log) &
```

Crontab Entry:

```
0 * * * * /path/to/async_cleanup.sh
```

Example 5: Daily Report Script (anacron and cron)

```
#!/bin/bash # daily_report.sh echo "Daily report
generated at $(date)" >> /var/log/daily_report.log
```

anacrontab Entry:

```
1 5 cron.daily run-parts /etc/cron.daily
```

Crontab Entry:

```
0 7 * * * /path/to/daily_report.sh
```

Integrating **cron** with **anacron** allows system administrators to run jobs consistently, even when the machine is not on. While **cron** is better for exact scheduling, **anacron** makes sure that jobs are finished even if the system was down. With these two components working together, we have a solid plan for automating different system functions, which will make system administration more efficient and dependable.

Using ‘grep’, ‘awk’ and ‘sed’

Text Processing and Manipulation Overview

Text processing and manipulation are critical tasks for system administrators. These tasks include searching for specific strings, extracting and transforming data, and automating the handling of configuration files, logs, and reports. Tools like **grep**, **awk**, and **sed** are powerful utilities for performing these tasks efficiently.

Tasks around Text Processing and Manipulation:

- Searching for specific patterns, errors, or events in log files.
- Extracting and modifying settings in configuration files.
- Extracting and summarizing data from structured text files.
- Generating reports by processing multiple files and formats.
- Formatting and restructuring text data for further processing or presentation.

Using ‘grep’ for Text Search

grep is used to search for specific patterns within files. It supports regular expressions for complex searches.

Example 1: Searching Log Files

Search for errors in the AlphaProject log file:

```
$ grep "ERROR" /var/log/alphaproject.log
```

Following is the output:

```
2024-05-20 10:00:00 ERROR: Failed to connect to database
2024-05-20 10:10:00 ERROR: Unauthorized access attempt
detected
```

Example 2: Case-Insensitive Search

Search for all instances of "backup" (case-insensitive) in the log file:

```
$ grep -i "backup" /var/log/alphaproject.log
```

Following is the output:

```
2024-05-20 11:00:00 Backup completed successfully 2024-
05-20 12:00:00 backup started
```

Example 3: Counting Matches

Count the number of error occurrences:

```
$ grep -c "ERROR" /var/log/alphaproject.log
```

Following is the output:

```
2
```

Using 'awk' for Data Extraction and Reporting

awk is a powerful text processing tool used for pattern scanning and processing. It is particularly useful for extracting specific fields from structured text files.

Example 1: Extracting Fields

Extract and display the timestamp and error messages from the log file:

```
$ awk '/ERROR/ {print $1, $2, $3, $4, $5, $6, $7, $8, $9,
$10}' /var/log/alphaproject.log
```

Following is the output:

```
2024-05-20 10:00:00 ERROR: Failed to connect to database
2024-05-20 10:10:00 ERROR: Unauthorized access attempt
detected
```

Example 2: Summarizing Data

Calculate the total disk usage for each user in a system:

```
$ awk '{usage[$1] += $3} END {for (user in usage) print user, usage[user]}' /var/log/disk_usage.log
```

Following is the output:

```
user1 2048 user2 1024 user3 512
```

Example 3: Formatting Output

Format the disk usage report for better readability:

```
$ awk '{usage[$1] += $3} END {printf "%-10s %10s\n", "User", "Disk Usage (MB)"; for (user in usage) printf "%-10s %10d\n", user, usage[user]}' /var/log/disk_usage.log
```

Following is the output:

```
User Disk Usage (MB) user1 2048 user2 1024 user3 512
```

Using 'sed' for Stream Editing and Text Manipulation

sed is a stream editor used for filtering and transforming text in a pipeline.

Example 1: Replacing Text

Replace all occurrences of "ERROR" with "WARNING" in the log file:

```
$ sed 's/ERROR/WARNING/g' /var/log/alphaproject.log
```

Following is the output:

```
2024-05-20 10:00:00 WARNING: Failed to connect to database 2024-05-20 10:10:00 WARNING: Unauthorized access attempt detected
```

Example 2: Deleting Lines

Delete all lines containing "DEBUG" from the log file:

```
$ sed '/DEBUG/d' /var/log/alphaproject.log
```

Following is the output:

```
2024-05-20 10:00:00 ERROR: Failed to connect to database
2024-05-20 10:10:00 ERROR: Unauthorized access attempt
detected
```

Example 3: Inserting Text

Insert a header line at the beginning of the file:

```
$ sed '1i\Timestamp\t\tMessage' /var/log/alphaproject.log
```

Following is the output:

```
Timestamp     Message 2024-05-20 10:00:00 ERROR: Failed
to connect to database 2024-05-20 10:10:00 ERROR:
Unauthorized access attempt detected
```

Sample Program: Performing Text Processing and Manipulation

Scenario 1: Log File Analysis with grep, awk, and sed

In this scenario, generate a report of error occurrences from the log file.

- Extract Error Lines:

```
$ grep "ERROR" /var/log/alphaproject.log >
/tmp/error_log.txt
```

- Summarize Errors by Timestamp:

```
$ awk '{print $1, $2, $3, $4, $5, $6, $7, $8, $9, $10}'
/tmp/error_log.txt
```

- Replace Error Text for Reporting:

```
$ sed 's/ERROR/WARNING/g' /tmp/error_log.txt
```

Following is the output:

```
2024-05-20 10:00:00 WARNING: Failed to connect to
database 2024-05-20 10:10:00 WARNING: Unauthorized access
attempt detected
```

Scenario 2: Configuration Management with awk and sed

In this scenario, update configuration settings in a file.

- Extract Current Configuration:

```
$ awk '/^Setting/ {print}' /etc/alphaproject/config.cfg
```

Following is the output:

```
Setting1=Value1 Setting2=Value2
```

- Modify Configuration Setting:

```
$ sed -i 's/Setting1=Value1/Setting1=NewValue/g'
/etc/alphaproject/config.cfg
```

- Verify Changes:

```
$ awk '/^Setting/ {print}' /etc/alphaproject/config.cfg
```

Following is the output:

```
Setting1=NewValue Setting2=Value2
```

Scenario 3: Automated Reporting with awk

In this scenario, generate a daily summary report of disk usage.

- Extract Disk Usage Data:

```
$ awk '{usage[$1] += $3} END {for (user in usage) print
user, usage[user]}' /var/log/disk_usage.log >
/tmp/disk_usage_summary.txt
```

- Format Report for Readability:

```
$ awk '{printf "%-10s %10d\n", $1, $2}'
/tmp/disk_usage_summary.txt > /tmp/disk_usage_report.txt
```

- Display Report:

```
$ cat /tmp/disk_usage_report.txt
```

Following is the output:

```
user1 2048 user2 1024 user3 512
```

Scenario 4: Data Transformation with awk and sed

In this scenario, transform and format data for analysis.

- Extract and Transform Data:

```
$ awk '{print $1, $2, $3}' /var/log/alphaproject.log |
sed 's/ /,/g' > /tmp/transformed_data.csv
```

- Format Data for Analysis:

```
$ awk 'BEGIN {print "Timestamp,Message"} {print}'
/tmp/transformed_data.csv > /tmp/formatted_data.csv
```

- Display Formatted Data:

```
$ cat /tmp/formatted_data.csv
```

Following is the output:

```
Timestamp,Message 2024-05-20,10:00:00,ERROR: Failed to
connect to database 2024-05-20,10:10:00,ERROR:
Unauthorized access attempt detected
```

When it comes to processing and manipulating text, system administrators have a lot of power and flexibility at their fingertips with **grep**, **awk**, and **sed**. These tools make it easy to search through log files, configuration files, and other text sources for data, extract it, transform it, and then report it. Because of this, it is easier to automate and manage systems, which guarantees that important data is handled and used efficiently.

Writing System Audit Scripts

System Auditing Overview

System administrators must do system audits to guarantee the optimal operation, compliance with policies, and security of Linux systems. User actions, system settings, installed applications, and security configurations are all potential audit targets. Security holes, configuration drifts, compliance infractions, and illegal access can all be found through auditing.

Common Auditing Tasks for System Administrators are as follows:

1. Tracking login attempts, user commands, and file access.
2. Verifying system configurations, network settings, and security policies.
3. Checking installed packages, software versions, and updates.
4. Ensuring proper permissions, firewall settings, and security patches.
5. Monitoring CPU, memory, disk usage, and network activity.

User Activity Auditing

Consider the objective is to monitor and log user login attempts and commands executed.

Following is the user activity script:

```
#!/bin/bash # user_activity_audit.sh
LOGFILE="/var/log/user_activity.log" echo "User Activity
Audit started at $(date)" >> $LOGFILE echo "Logged in
users:" >> $LOGFILE who >> $LOGFILE echo "Last login
attempts:" >> $LOGFILE last -n 5 >> $LOGFILE echo "Recent
command executions:" >> $LOGFILE for user in $(cut -f1 -
d: /etc/passwd); do if [ -f /home/$user/.bash_history ];
then echo "Commands executed by $user:" >> $LOGFILE tail
-n 10 /home/$user/.bash_history >> $LOGFILE fi done echo
"User Activity Audit completed at $(date)" >> $LOGFILE
```

In the above code snippet,

- LOGFILE: Specifies the log file where audit information will be recorded.
- who: Lists currently logged-in users.
- last: Displays recent login attempts.
- .bash_history: Contains the command history for each user.

Running the script:

```
$ chmod +x user_activity_audit.sh $
./user_activity_audit.sh
```

Following is the output (in log file):

```
User Activity Audit started at Mon May 20 10:00:00 UTC
2024 Logged in users: user1 pts/0 2024-05-20 09:00 (:0)
user2 pts/1 2024-05-20 09:15 (:1) Last login attempts:
user1 pts/0 :0 Mon May 20 09:00 still logged in user2
pts/1 :1 Mon May 20 09:15 still logged in ... Recent
command executions: Commands executed by user1: cd /var
ls -la ... User Activity Audit completed at Mon May 20
10:01:00 UTC 2024
```

Configuration Auditing

Now, consider the objective is to verify system and network configurations.

Following is the configuration audit script:

```
#!/bin/bash # configuration_audit.sh
LOGFILE="/var/log/configuration_audit.log" echo
"Configuration Audit started at $(date)" >> $LOGFILE echo
"Checking /etc/passwd for unauthorized changes:" >>
$LOGFILE md5sum /etc/passwd >> $LOGFILE echo "Checking
/etc/ssh/sshd_config for modifications:" >> $LOGFILE
md5sum /etc/ssh/sshd_config >> $LOGFILE echo "Network
configuration:" >> $LOGFILE ifconfig >> $LOGFILE echo
"Active listening ports:" >> $LOGFILE netstat -tuln >>
$LOGFILE echo "Firewall settings:" >> $LOGFILE iptables -
L >> $LOGFILE echo "Configuration Audit completed at
$(date)" >> $LOGFILE
```

In the above code snippet,

- md5sum: Generates an MD5 checksum for files to detect changes.
- ifconfig: Displays network configuration.
- netstat: Lists active listening ports.
- iptables: Shows current firewall settings.

Running the script:

```
$ chmod +x configuration_audit.sh $
./configuration_audit.sh
```

Following is the output (in log file):

```
Configuration Audit started at Mon May 20 10:10:00 UTC
2024 Checking /etc/passwd for unauthorized changes:
d41d8cd98f00b204e9800998ecf8427e /etc/passwd Checking
/etc/ssh/sshd_config for modifications:
d41d8cd98f00b204e9800998ecf8427e /etc/ssh/sshd_config
Network configuration: eth0 Link encap:Ethernet HWaddr
00:0c:29:68:22:5b inet addr:192.168.1.100
Bcast:192.168.1.255 Mask:255.255.255.0 ... Active
listening ports: tcp 0 0 0.0.0.0:22 0.0.0.0:* LISTEN ...
Firewall settings: Chain INPUT (policy ACCEPT) target
prot opt source destination ... Configuration Audit
completed at Mon May 20 10:11:00 UTC 2024
```

Software Auditing

What if we want to check installed packages and software versions?

Following is the software audit script:

```
#!/bin/bash # software_audit.sh
LOGFILE="/var/log/software_audit.log" echo "Software
Audit started at $(date)" >> $LOGFILE echo "List of
installed packages:" >> $LOGFILE dpkg -l >> $LOGFILE echo
"Checking for available updates:" >> $LOGFILE apt-get
update -qq apt-get upgrade -s | grep "^Inst" >> $LOGFILE
echo "Software Audit completed at $(date)" >> $LOGFILE
```

In the above code snippet,

- dpkg -l: Lists installed packages.
- apt-get update -qq: Updates the package list quietly.
- apt-get upgrade -s: Simulates the upgrade to check for available updates.

Running the script:

```
$ chmod +x software_audit.sh $ ./software_audit.sh
```

Following is the output (in log file):

```
Software Audit started at Mon May 20 10:20:00 UTC 2024
List of installed packages: ii acl 2.2.53-4 amd64 Access
control list utilities ii adduser 3.118 all add and
remove users and groups ... Checking for available
updates: Inst libapt-pkg5.0 [1.4.9] (1.4.10
Ubuntu:18.04/bionic [amd64]) Inst libgnutls30 [3.5.18-
1ubuntu1.3] (3.5.18-1ubuntu1.4 Ubuntu:18.04/bionic-
updates [amd64]) ... Software Audit completed at Mon May
20 10:21:00 UTC 2024
```

Security Auditing

And, assume if we want to verify file permissions and security settings.

Following is the security audit script:

```
#!/bin/bash # security_audit.sh
LOGFILE="/var/log/security_audit.log" echo "Security
Audit started at $(date)" >> $LOGFILE echo "Checking
permissions of sensitive files:" >> $LOGFILE ls -l
/etc/passwd /etc/shadow /etc/ssh/sshd_config >> $LOGFILE
echo "Checking for world-writable files:" >> $LOGFILE
find / -xdev -type f -perm -0002 >> $LOGFILE echo
"Checking for SUID/SGID files:" >> $LOGFILE find / -type
f \( -perm -4000 -o -perm -2000 \) -exec ls -l {} \; >>
$LOGFILE echo "Security Audit completed at $(date)" >>
$LOGFILE
```

In the above code snippet,

- ls -l: Lists detailed file information, including permissions.
- find / -xdev -type f -perm -0002: Finds world-writable files.
- find / -type f
- $-perm-4000-o-perm-2000$
- $-perm-4000-o-perm-2000$: Finds files with SUID or SGID set.

Running the script:

```
$ chmod +x security_audit.sh $ ./security_audit.sh
```

Following is the output (in log file):

```
Security Audit started at Mon May 20 10:30:00 UTC 2024
Checking permissions of sensitive files: -rw-r--r-- 1
root root 2383 Apr 20 15:32 /etc/passwd -rw------- 1 root
root 1369 Apr 20 15:32 /etc/shadow -rw-r--r-- 1 root root
1864 Apr 20 15:32 /etc/ssh/sshd_config Checking for
world-writable files: /tmp/testfile ... Checking for
SUID/SGID files: -rwsr-xr-x 1 root root 97704 Feb 2 2019
/usr/bin/sudo ... Security Audit completed at Mon May 20
10:31:00 UTC 2024
```

Resource Usage Auditing

Very commonly, we want to monitor CPU, memory, and disk usage.

Following is the resource usage audit script:

```
#!/bin/bash # resource_usage_audit.sh
LOGFILE="/var/log/resource_usage_audit.log" echo
"Resource Usage Audit started at $(date)" >> $LOGFILE
echo "CPU Usage:" >> $LOGFILE mpstat >> $LOGFILE echo
"Memory Usage:" >> $LOGFILE free -m >> $LOGFILE echo
"Disk Usage:" >> $LOGFILE df -h >> $LOGFILE echo "Network
Usage:" >> $LOGFILE ifstat -t >> $LOGFILE echo "Resource
Usage Audit completed at $(date)" >> $LOGFILE
```

In the above code snippet,

- mpstat: Reports CPU usage.
- free -m: Displays memory usage.
- df -h: Shows disk usage in a human-readable format.
- ifstat -t: Displays network interface statistics with a timestamp.

Running the script:

```
$ chmod +x resource_usage_audit.sh $
./resource_usage_audit.sh
```

Following is the output (in log file):

```
Resource Usage Audit started at Mon May 20 10:40:00 UTC
2024 CPU Usage: Linux 4.15.0-47-generic (alphaproject)
05/20/2024 _x86_64_ (2 CPU) 08:40:00 AM CPU %usr %nice
%sys %iowait %irq %soft %steal %guest %idle 08:40:00 AM
all 5.06 0.00 1.27 0.38 0.00 0.10 0.00 0.00 93.20 Memory
Usage: total used free shared buff/cache available Mem:
7962 1853 3158 179 2951 5601 Swap: 2047 0 2047 Disk
Usage: Filesystem Size Used Avail Use% Mounted on udev
3.9G 0 3.9G 0% /dev tmpfs 796M 1.1M 795M 1% /run
/dev/sda1 50G 12G 36G 25% / ... Network Usage: Interface
RX Pkts/Rate TX Pkts/Rate RX Data/Rate TX Data/Rate eth0
385474 180557 47845460 12345678 ... Resource Usage Audit
completed at Mon May 20 10:41:00 UTC 2024
```

A secure and functional system is maintained by recognizing and swiftly correcting issues with the stated above audit scripts. Incorporating **grep**, **awk**, and **sed** into these scripts improves their data processing and analysis capabilities.

Automated Scripts for Backup and Recovery

Creating automated scripts for backup and recovery is essential to ensure data integrity and availability without the need for constant sysadmin intervention. This section will cover writing scripts that perform regular backups and automate recovery processes, including setting up alerts to trigger recovery actions.

Backup Script

Think if we want to automate the backup of the AlphaProject directory to ensure data is regularly saved.

Following is the backup script:

```
#!/bin/bash # automated_backup.sh
SOURCE_DIR="/var/www/alphaproject"
BACKUP_DIR="/backup/alphaproject" TIMESTAMP=$(date
+%Y%m%d%H%M%S) BACKUP_FILE="$BACKUP_DIR/backup-
$TIMESTAMP.tar.gz" LOGFILE="/var/log/backup.log" echo
"Backup started at $(date)" >> $LOGFILE # Create backup
directory if it doesn't exist mkdir -p $BACKUP_DIR #
Perform the backup tar -czf $BACKUP_FILE $SOURCE_DIR #
Check if the backup was successful if [ $? -eq 0 ]; then
echo "Backup completed successfully at $(date)" >>
$LOGFILE else echo "Backup failed at $(date)" >> $LOGFILE
exit 1 fi # Clean up old backups (older than 7 days) find
$BACKUP_DIR -type f -mtime +7 -name "*.tar.gz" -exec rm
{} \; echo "Old backups cleaned up at $(date)" >>
$LOGFILE
```

In the above code snippet,

- Variables: Define source directory, backup directory, timestamp, and log file.
- Commands:
  - **mkdir -p $BACKUP_DIR**: Ensure the backup directory exists.
  - **tar -czf $BACKUP_FILE $SOURCE_DIR**: Create a compressed archive of the source directory.
  - **find $BACKUP_DIR -type f -mtime +7 -name "*.tar.gz" -exec rm {} \;**: Delete backups older than 7 days.

Running the script:

```
$ chmod +x automated_backup.sh $ ./automated_backup.sh
```

Crontab Entry:

```
0 2 * * * /path/to/automated_backup.sh
```

This entry schedules the backup script to run daily at 2 AM.

Recovery Script

What if we want to automate the most repetitive task of running the recovery process from the latest backup?

Following is the recovery script:

```
#!/bin/bash # automated_recovery.sh
BACKUP_DIR="/backup/alphaproject"
RESTORE_DIR="/var/www/alphaproject"
LOGFILE="/var/log/recovery.log" echo "Recovery started at
$(date)" >> $LOGFILE # Find the latest backup file
LATEST_BACKUP=$(ls -t $BACKUP_DIR/*.tar.gz | head -n 1)
if [ -z "$LATEST_BACKUP" ]; then echo "No backup file
found" >> $LOGFILE exit 1 fi # Extract the backup file
tar -xzf $LATEST_BACKUP -C / # Check if the extraction
was successful if [ $? -eq 0 ]; then echo "Recovery
completed successfully at $(date)" >> $LOGFILE else echo
"Recovery failed at $(date)" >> $LOGFILE exit 1 fi
```

In the above code snippet,

- Variables: Define backup directory, restore directory, and log file.
- Commands:
    - ls -t $BACKUP_DIR/*.tar.gz | head -n 1: Find the latest backup file.
    - tar -xzf $LATEST_BACKUP -C /: Extract the latest backup archive to the root directory.

Running the script:

```
$ chmod +x automated_recovery.sh $
./automated_recovery.sh
```

Setting up Alerts to Trigger Recovery

If we want to automatically trigger the recovery script when a failure is detected.

Following is the sample monitoring script:

```
#!/bin/bash # monitor_and_recover.sh
LOGFILE="/var/log/monitor.log"
RECOVERY_SCRIPT="/path/to/automated_recovery.sh" echo
"Monitoring started at $(date)" >> $LOGFILE # Check if
the web server is running if ! systemctl is-active --
quiet apache2; then echo "Web server is down at $(date)"
>> $LOGFILE # Trigger the recovery script
$RECOVERY_SCRIPT if [ $? -eq 0 ]; then echo "Recovery
triggered successfully at $(date)" >> $LOGFILE else echo
"Recovery failed to trigger at $(date)" >> $LOGFILE fi
else echo "Web server is running at $(date)" >> $LOGFILE
fi
```

In the above code snippet,

- Variables: Define log file and path to the recovery script.
- Commands:
    - **systemctl is-active --quiet apache2**: Check if the web server is active.
    - **$RECOVERY_SCRIPT**: Execute the recovery script if the web server is down.

Running the script:

```
$ chmod +x monitor_and_recover.sh $
./monitor_and_recover.sh
```

Scheduling the Script Monitoring with cron

Crontab Entry:

```
*/5 * * * * /path/to/monitor_and_recover.sh
```

This entry schedules the monitoring script to run every 5 minutes.

Automated recovery scripts guarantee rapid restoration in the event of problems, while regular backups protect against data loss. In order to keep the system running smoothly and reliably, monitoring scripts are essential for finding problems and initiating recovery.

Summary

You learned the significance of automation in system administration in this chapter, with an emphasis on shell scripting as a means to streamline and improve a variety of duties. An introduction to shell scripting was provided at the beginning of the chapter, outlining its advantages such as consistency, efficiency, and the capacity to automate complicated activities. After that, you delved into the basics of scripting to automate routine AlphaProject operations like checking the health of a network, managing users, monitoring disk consumption, automating directory backups, and system updates.

In order to achieve more adaptable and dynamic automation, the chapter moved on to learning script variables and control structures. You gained knowledge of how to include variables into scripts for data storage and reuse, as well as control structures for conditional decision-making and action repetition, such as if-else statements, loops, and case statements. Next, we went over how to manage task automation, including how to use cron for activities that need to run at regular intervals or at set times and anacron for systems that aren't constantly on. Hourly, weekly, and annual task scheduling and asynchronous task management are some real-world examples.

To further explore text processing and modification, the chapter delves into the use of grep, awk, and sed to search, extract, and alter data from various text sources such as configuration files, log files, and more. There was a heavy emphasis on system audits as well, with scripts supplied to check user actions, system settings, program installations, security configurations, and resource use. Lastly, the chapter went over how to make backup and recovery scripts automatically, which is a better way to make sure your data is safe and always available.

CHAPTER 7: ADVANCED SYSTEM ADMINISTRATION

Introduction

Navigating large-scale Linux systems is the focus of this chapter. Readers interested in learning more about Kubernetes, cluster management, load balancing, and kernel customization—as well as large-scale deployments—will find this chapter to be a fantastic resource.

In the first section, "Managing Large-Scale Deployments," you will learn about methods and resources for effectively distributing programs and services over a network of computers. The methods and tools for automation that guarantee regular and dependable deployments will be covered in this chapter. Following this, the section "Up and Running with Kubernetes" will provide an introduction to Kubernetes, a robust platform for container orchestration. Here, we will go over the fundamentals of containerized application management, including how to install and configure it. The groundwork for more complex Kubernetes operations will be laid out in this section. Practical insights into setting up and handling clusters, whether for Kubernetes or other distributed systems, will be provided in the next section 'Setting up and Managing Clusters'. The design, implementation, and upkeep of clusters, with an emphasis on high availability and scalability, will also be covered in this chapter.

The next section 'Implementing Load Balancing' will cover the techniques and tools used to distribute network traffic across multiple servers, thereby accommodating fluctuating loads and guaranteeing uninterrupted service access. Lastly, in Customizing the Kernel, we will look at how to modify the Linux kernel to fit our needs. The goal of this extensive chapter is to provide you the tools needed to administer complex and large-scale Linux setups.

Managing Large-Scale Deployments

Managing large-scale deployments involves handling numerous servers, applications, and services efficiently and consistently. These deployments require careful planning, automation, and monitoring to ensure reliability, scalability, and maintainability.

Practical Deployment of AlphaProject at a Large Scale

Infrastructure Planning

Before deploying AlphaProject at a large scale, plan the infrastructure. Identify the number of servers, network architecture, storage requirements, and load distribution.

- Servers: Determine the number of servers required based on expected load.
- Network Architecture: Design a network layout that includes load balancers, application servers, and databases.
- Storage: Plan for distributed storage to handle data across multiple servers.

Configuration Management with Ansible

Use a configuration management tool like Ansible to automate the setup and configuration of servers.

- Installing Ansible:

```
$ sudo apt update $ sudo apt install ansible
```

- Creating an Inventory File:

```
# /etc/ansible/hosts [webservers] web1.gitforgits.com
web2.gitforgits.com [databases] db1.gitforgits.com
db2.gitforgits.com
```

- Creating a Playbook:

```
# deploy.yml - hosts: webservers tasks: - name: Install
Apache apt: name: apache2 state: present - name: Deploy
AlphaProject Code copy: src: /local/path/alphaproject/
dest: /var/www/alphaproject/ owner: www-data group: www-
data mode: '0755'
```

- Running the Playbook:

```
$ ansible-playbook deploy.yml
```

Automated Deployment with Jenkins

Use Jenkins for continuous integration and continuous deployment (CI/CD). Jenkins automates building, testing, and deploying code.

- Installing Jenkins:

```
$ sudo apt update $ sudo apt install openjdk-11-jdk $
wget -q -O - https://pkg.jenkins.io/debian/jenkins.io.key
| sudo apt-key add - $ sudo sh -c 'echo deb
http://pkg.jenkins.io/debian-stable binary/ >
/etc/apt/sources.list.d/jenkins.list' $ sudo apt update $
sudo apt install jenkins $ sudo systemctl start jenkins $
sudo systemctl enable jenkins
```

- Setting up a Jenkins Job:
  - Create a New Job: Go to Jenkins dashboard, click on "New Item," name the job, and select "Freestyle project."
  - Source Code Management: Configure the repository from which Jenkins will pull the code (e.g., Git).
  - Build Triggers: Set up triggers like "Poll SCM" or "Build periodically."
  - Build Steps: Add build steps, such as shell scripts to deploy the project.

Following is the sample of the build script:

```
#!/bin/bash ansible-playbook /path/to/deploy.yml
```

Load Balancing with HAProxy

Use HAProxy to distribute traffic across multiple servers, ensuring no single server is overwhelmed.

- Installing HAProxy:

```
$ sudo apt update $ sudo apt install haproxy
```

- Configuring HAProxy:

```
$ sudo nano /etc/haproxy/haproxy.cfg
```

Following is the sample configuration:

```
frontend http_front bind *:80 stats uri /haproxy?stats
default_backend http_back backend http_back balance
roundrobin server web1 web1.gitforgits.com:80 check
server web2 web2.gitforgits.com:80 check
```

- Restarting HAProxy:

```
$ sudo systemctl restart haproxy
```

Continuous Monitoring with Prometheus and Grafana

Implement monitoring to keep track of server health, application performance, and other critical metrics.

- Installing Prometheus:

```
$ sudo useradd --no-create-home --shell /bin/false
prometheus $ sudo mkdir /etc/prometheus $ sudo mkdir
/var/lib/prometheus $ sudo chown prometheus:prometheus
/etc/prometheus /var/lib/prometheus $ wget
https://github.com/prometheus/prometheus/releases/downloa
d/v2.26.0/prometheus-2.26.0.linux-amd64.tar.gz $ tar -xvf
prometheus-2.26.0.linux-amd64.tar.gz $ sudo cp
prometheus-2.26.0.linux-amd64/prometheus /usr/local/bin/
$ sudo cp prometheus-2.26.0.linux-amd64/promtool
/usr/local/bin/ $ sudo cp -r prometheus-2.26.0.linux-
amd64/consoles /etc/prometheus $ sudo cp -r prometheus-
2.26.0.linux-amd64/console_libraries /etc/prometheus $
sudo cp prometheus-2.26.0.linux-amd64/prometheus.yml
/etc/prometheus $ sudo chown -R prometheus:prometheus
/etc/prometheus /var/lib/prometheus $ sudo nano
/etc/systemd/system/prometheus.service
```

- Prometheus Service File:

```
[Unit] Description=Prometheus Wants=network-online.target
After=network-online.target [Service] User=prometheus
Group=prometheus Type=simple
ExecStart=/usr/local/bin/prometheus --config.file
/etc/prometheus/prometheus.yml --storage.tsdb.path
/var/lib/prometheus/ [Install] WantedBy=multi-user.target
```

- Starting Prometheus:

```
$ sudo systemctl daemon-reload $ sudo systemctl start
prometheus $ sudo systemctl enable prometheus
```

- Installing Grafana:

```
$ wget
https://dl.grafana.com/oss/release/grafana_7.4.3_amd64.de
b $ sudo dpkg -i grafana_7.4.3_amd64.deb $ sudo systemctl
start grafana-server $ sudo systemctl enable grafana-
server
```

- Configuring Grafana to Use Prometheus:
  - Login to Grafana: Default port is 3000 (http://your_server_ip:3000).
  - Add Data Source: In Grafana, go to Configuration -> Data Sources -> Add data source -> Prometheus.
  - Set URL: Point to your Prometheus server (http://localhost:9090).

Ensuring High Availability and Redundancy

Set up replication for databases to ensure data availability and redundancy. Consider an example of MySQL Replication:

- On Master Server:

```
CREATE USER 'replicator'@'%' IDENTIFIED BY 'password';
GRANT REPLICATION SLAVE ON *.* TO 'replicator'@'%'; FLUSH
PRIVILEGES; SHOW MASTER STATUS;
```

- On Slave Server:

```
CHANGE MASTER TO MASTER_HOST='master_ip',
MASTER_USER='replicator', MASTER_PASSWORD='password',
MASTER_LOG_FILE='mysql-bin.000001', MASTER_LOG_POS=120;
START SLAVE; SHOW SLAVE STATUS\G
```

- Use multiple load balancers and configure them for failover.
- Install Keepalived:

```
$ sudo apt update $ sudo apt install keepalived
```

- Configure Keepalived:

```
$ sudo nano /etc/keepalived/keepalived.conf
```

Following is the sample configuration:

```
vrrp_script chk_haproxy { script "killall -0 haproxy"
interval 2 } vrrp_instance VI_1 { interface eth0 state
MASTER virtual_router_id 51 priority 100 advert_int 1
authentication { auth_type PASS auth_pass 1234 }
virtual_ipaddress { 192.168.1.100 } track_script {
chk_haproxy } }
```

- Restart Keepalived:

```
$ sudo systemctl restart keepalived
```

Make sure the failover methods are ready to handle a real failure by testing them often. Ansible, Jenkins, load balancing, and Grafana are some of the tools that sysadmins use to manage configurations and ensure that the AlphaProject is deployed consistently, efficiently, and with high availability. Deployments are made even more reliable and scalable using redundancy and failover techniques, which guarantee excellent performance with little downtime.

Up and Running with Kubernetes

Kubernetes Overview

Kubernetes, often referred to as K8s, is an open-source platform designed to automate the deployment, scaling, and management of containerized applications. Developed by Google, Kubernetes has revolutionized the way applications are deployed and managed, providing a robust framework for running distributed systems resiliently.

Key Features of Kubernetes:

- Kubernetes can manage your deployment to ensure that your application is always running the latest version.
- Restarts containers that fail, replaces and reschedules them when nodes die, kills containers that don't respond to user-defined health checks, and doesn't advertise them to clients until they are ready to serve.
- Scale your application up and down with a simple command, with a UI, or automatically based on CPU usage.
- No need to modify your application to use an unfamiliar service discovery mechanism.
- Automatically mount the storage system of your choice, whether from local storage, a public cloud provider, or a network storage system.

Installing and Configuring Kubernetes

To set up Kubernetes on your existing development environment, follow these steps:

Installing Docker

Kubernetes uses Docker as its container runtime.

```
$ sudo apt update $ sudo apt install -y apt-transport-
https ca-certificates curl software-properties-common $
curl -fsSL https://download.docker.com/linux/ubuntu/gpg |
sudo apt-key add - $ sudo add-apt-repository "deb
[arch=amd64] https://download.docker.com/linux/ubuntu
$(lsb_release -cs) stable" $ sudo apt update $ sudo apt
install -y docker-ce $ sudo systemctl enable docker $
sudo systemctl start docker
```

Installing kubeadm, kubelet, and kubectl

`kubeadm` helps you set up a Kubernetes cluster, **`kubelet`** runs on all the machines in your cluster and does things like starting pods and containers, and **`kubectl`** is the command-line tool to interact with your cluster.

```
$ sudo apt update $ sudo apt install -y apt-transport-
https curl $ curl -s
https://packages.cloud.google.com/apt/doc/apt-key.gpg |
sudo apt-key add - $ sudo apt-add-repository "deb
http://apt.kubernetes.io/ kubernetes-xenial main" $ sudo
apt update $ sudo apt install -y kubelet kubeadm kubectl
$ sudo apt-mark hold kubelet kubeadm kubectl
```

Initializing Master Node

Run the following command on the master node to initialize the Kubernetes cluster:

```
$ sudo kubeadm init --pod-network-cidr=192.168.0.0/16
```

After running this command, you will see a **kubeadm join** command in the output. Save this command as it will be used to join worker nodes to the cluster.

Setting up kubectl for Master Node

To start using your cluster, you need to set up the **kubectl** configuration:

```
$ mkdir -p $HOME/.kube $ sudo cp -i
/etc/kubernetes/admin.conf $HOME/.kube/config $ sudo
chown $(id -u):$(id -g) $HOME/.kube/config
```

Installing Pod Network Add-on

A pod network allows communication between the nodes in the cluster. For this, we will use Calico:

```
$ kubectl apply -f
https://docs.projectcalico.org/manifests/calico.yaml
```

Joining Worker Nodes

Run the **kubeadm join** command you saved earlier on each worker node to join them to the cluster:

```
$ sudo kubeadm join <master-node-ip>:6443 --token <token>
--discovery-token-ca-cert-hash sha256:<hash>
```

Verifying Cluster

Check the status of your nodes:

```
$ kubectl get nodes
```

You should see the master and worker nodes listed with a **Ready** status.

Deploying an Application

Now, We shall deploy a simple Nginx application to verify the setup.

- Creating a Deployment:

```
$ kubectl create deployment nginx --image=nginx
```

- Exposing the Deployment:

```
$ kubectl expose deployment nginx --port=80 --
type=NodePort
```

- Checking the Deployment:

```
$ kubectl get pods $ kubectl get svc
```

Access the Nginx application using the NodePort value displayed in the service details.

Scaling the Application

To demonstrate Kubernetes' scaling capabilities, scale the Nginx deployment:

```
$ kubectl scale deployment nginx --replicas=3 $ kubectl
get pods
```

You may observe that Kubernetes has launched extra Nginx pods. Once the cluster is configured, it becomes easy to deploy, expose, and grow applications. This highlights the flexibility and power of Kubernetes in managing distributed systems on a wide scale.

Setting up and Managing Clusters

Exploring Clusters

A cluster is a collection of computers that share resources and operate as an integrated whole. In order to guarantee high availability, redundancy, and improved performance, clusters are utilized. One or more worker nodes and one or more master nodes make up a cluster in Kubernetes. Workers take care of workloads, while the master node oversees all of the worker nodes and the containers (pods) that operate on them.

Components of a Kubernetes Cluster:

- Master Node: The control plane that manages the cluster.
    - kube-apiserver: Exposes the Kubernetes API.
    - etcd: A distributed key-value store used for configuration data.
    - kube-scheduler: Schedules the pods on the worker nodes.
    - kube-controller-manager: Runs controller processes to regulate the state of the cluster.
    - cloud-controller-manager: Manages cloud-specific controller logic.
- Worker Nodes: Execute the containers.
    - kubelet: Ensures that containers are running in a pod.
    - kube-proxy: Maintains network rules for pod communication.
    - Container Runtime: Runs the containers (e.g., Docker).

Sample Program: Setting up and Managing Clusters

Preparing the Infrastructure

Ensure you have multiple machines (virtual or physical) ready to be part of the cluster. For this example, we shall assume you have three machines: one master and two worker nodes. And, ensure the following:

- All nodes should be running Ubuntu 18.04 or later.
- Each node should have a static IP address.
- Ensure that the machines can communicate with each other over the network.

Installing Docker

Install Docker on all nodes (master and worker nodes):

```
$ sudo apt update $ sudo apt install -y apt-transport-
https ca-certificates curl software-properties-common $
curl -fsSL https://download.docker.com/linux/ubuntu/gpg |
sudo apt-key add - $ sudo add-apt-repository "deb
[arch=amd64] https://download.docker.com/linux/ubuntu
$(lsb_release -cs) stable" $ sudo apt update $ sudo apt
install -y docker-ce $ sudo systemctl enable docker $
sudo systemctl start docker
```

Installing kubeadm, kubelet, and kubectl

Install these tools on all nodes:

```
$ sudo apt update $ sudo apt install -y apt-transport-
https curl $ curl -s
https://packages.cloud.google.com/apt/doc/apt-key.gpg |
sudo apt-key add - $ sudo apt-add-repository "deb
http://apt.kubernetes.io/ kubernetes-xenial main" $ sudo
apt update $ sudo apt install -y kubelet kubeadm kubectl
$ sudo apt-mark hold kubelet kubeadm kubectl
```

Initializing the Master Node

On the master node, initialize the cluster:

```
$ sudo kubeadm init --pod-network-cidr=192.168.0.0/16
```

After the initialization completes, you will see a **`kubeadm join`** command in the output. Save this command as you will use it to join the worker nodes to the cluster.

Then, setting up kubectl for the Master Node:

```
$ mkdir -p $HOME/.kube $ sudo cp -i
/etc/kubernetes/admin.conf $HOME/.kube/config $ sudo
chown $(id -u):$(id -g) $HOME/.kube/config
```

Installing Pod Network Add-on

Install a network add-on for communication between the nodes. For this, we will use Calico:

```
$ kubectl apply -f
https://docs.projectcalico.org/manifests/calico.yaml
```

Joining Worker Nodes to the Cluster

Run the **kubeadm join** command saved from the master node initialization on each worker node to join them to the cluster:

```
$ sudo kubeadm join <master-node-ip>:6443 --token <token>
--discovery-token-ca-cert-hash sha256:<hash>
```

Verifying the Cluster

On the master node, check the status of the nodes:

```
$ kubectl get nodes
```

You should see all the nodes (master and workers) listed with a **Ready** status.

Deploying AlphaProject on Cluster

Now that the cluster is set up, we shall deploy the AlphaProject application on it.

Creating a Deployment for AlphaProject

- Create a deployment YAML file for AlphaProject:

```
# alphaproject-deployment.yaml apiVersion: apps/v1 kind:
Deployment metadata: name: alphaproject spec: replicas: 3
selector: matchLabels: app: alphaproject template:
metadata: labels: app: alphaproject spec: containers: -
name: alphaproject image: alphaproject/image:latest
ports: - containerPort: 80
```

- Apply the deployment:

```
$ kubectl apply -f alphaproject-deployment.yaml
```

Exposing the Deployment

- Create a service to expose the AlphaProject deployment:

```
# alphaproject-service.yaml apiVersion: v1 kind: Service
metadata: name: alphaproject-service spec: selector: app:
alphaproject ports: - protocol: TCP port: 80 targetPort:
80 type: NodePort
```

- Apply the service:

```
$ kubectl apply -f alphaproject-service.yaml
```

Verifying the Deployment

- Check the status of the deployment and the service:

```
$ kubectl get deployments $ kubectl get pods $ kubectl
get svc
```

- You should see the AlphaProject deployment running with the specified number of replicas and the service exposing it.

Scaling the AlphaProject Deployment

To demonstrate the scaling capabilities, let us witness how the AlphaProject deployment is scaled:

```
$ kubectl scale deployment alphaproject --replicas=5 $
kubectl get pods
```

Kubernetes will automatically start additional pods for the AlphaProject, distributing them across the worker nodes.

Monitoring the Cluster

Use Kubernetes built-in tools and third-party solutions like Prometheus and Grafana to monitor the cluster's health and performance.

For example, let us consider,

- Checking Node and Pod Status:

```
$ kubectl get nodes $ kubectl get pods --all-namespaces
```

- Describing Resources:

```
$ kubectl describe node <node-name> $ kubectl describe
pod <pod-name>
```

- Viewing Logs:

```
$ kubectl logs <pod-name>
```

As a sysadmin, you can quickly set up a Kubernetes cluster using tools like kubeadm, kubectl, and network add-ons like Calico. Kubernetes simplifies application deployment and management with its robust features for application scaling, monitoring, and maintenance, as well as with other apps like AlphaProject. Taking this approach allows sysadmins to efficiently and dependably manage installations on a big scale.

Implementing Load Balancing

Introduction to Load Balancers

When deploying on a big scale, load balancers play an essential role in distributing application or network traffic among numerous servers. To improve availability, dependability, and performance, load balancing primarily aims to prevent any one server from becoming a bottleneck. Layer 4 (transport) and Layer 7 (application) are two examples of the network stack layers at which load balancers can function.

Types of Load Balancers

1. Hardware Load Balancers: Physical devices that distribute traffic.
2. Software Load Balancers: Software solutions running on standard hardware.
3. DNS Load Balancing: Using DNS to distribute traffic across multiple IP addresses.

Common Algorithms

1. Round Robin: Distributes traffic equally across all servers.
2. Least Connections: Directs traffic to the server with the fewest active connections.
3. IP Hash: Uses the client's IP address to determine which server receives the request.

Monitoring System Load

Before implementing load balancing, it is crucial to monitor the system load to understand traffic patterns and identify potential bottlenecks. Tools such as **`top`**, **`htop`**, **`vmstat`**, and **`iostat`** are commonly used for monitoring system load in Linux.

- Using **`top`** and **`htop`** to Monitor System Load:

```
$ top $ htop
```

- Using **`vmstat`** to Monitor System Performance:

```
$ vmstat 1 10
```

- Using **`iostat`** to Monitor Disk I/O:

```
$ iostat -xz 1 10
```

These commands provide real-time insights into CPU usage, memory usage, process statistics, and disk I/O, helping sysadmins determine if load balancing is necessary.

Sample Program: Load Balancing using HAProxy

One of the most well-known open-source software load balancers, HAProxy, has multiple load balancing methods and can manage many concurrent connections. Following is the process for configuring HAProxy to provide load balancing:

Installing HAProxy

```
$ sudo apt update $ sudo apt install haproxy
```

Configuring HAProxy

Edit the HAProxy configuration file to set up load balancing. The default configuration file is located at **`/etc/haproxy/haproxy.cfg`**.

Given below is the example of the configuration:

```
global log /dev/log local0 log /dev/log local1 notice
chroot /var/lib/haproxy stats socket
/run/haproxy/admin.sock mode 660 level admin expose-fd
listeners stats timeout 30s user haproxy group haproxy
daemon defaults log global mode http option httplog
option dontlognull timeout connect 5000 timeout client
50000 timeout server 50000 errorfile 400
/etc/haproxy/errors/400.http errorfile 403
/etc/haproxy/errors/403.http errorfile 408
/etc/haproxy/errors/408.http errorfile 500
/etc/haproxy/errors/500.http errorfile 502
/etc/haproxy/errors/502.http errorfile 503
/etc/haproxy/errors/503.http errorfile 504
/etc/haproxy/errors/504.http frontend http_front bind
*:80 stats uri /haproxy?stats default_backend http_back
backend http_back balance roundrobin server web1
192.168.1.101:80 check server web2 192.168.1.102:80 check
```

In the above code snippet,

- frontend http_front: Defines the front-end configuration listening on port 80.
- backend http_back: Defines the back-end servers and the load balancing algorithm (round robin).
- server web1 192.168.1.101:80 check: Specifies a back-end server with health check enabled.

Restarting HAProxy

Apply the configuration changes by restarting HAProxy:

```
$ sudo systemctl restart haproxy
```

Verifying Load Balancer Configuration

To ensure the load balancer is working correctly, access the HAProxy statistics page or use curl to simulate traffic.

```
$ for i in {1..10}; do curl -I http://<your_server_ip>;
done
```

Observe the distribution of requests across the back-end servers.

Advanced Load Balancing

Using Least Connections Algorithm

Modify the backend section in the HAProxy configuration to use the least connections algorithm:

```
backend http_back balance leastconn server web1
192.168.1.101:80 check server web2 192.168.1.102:80 check
```

Load Balancing with SSL Termination

To handle SSL termination at the load balancer, update the HAProxy configuration:

```
frontend https_front bind *:443 ssl crt
/etc/haproxy/certs/site.pem default_backend http_back
backend http_back balance roundrobin server web1
192.168.1.101:80 check server web2 192.168.1.102:80 check
```

Generate SSL Certificates

Use Let's Encrypt or OpenSSL to generate SSL certificates. Following is the example with Let's Encrypt:

```
$ sudo apt-get install certbot $ sudo certbot certonly --
standalone -d yourdomain.com
```

Update the **bind** directive in HAProxy to point to the generated certificates.

Health Checks and Failover

HAProxy performs health checks to ensure back-end servers are available. If a server fails the health check, it is automatically removed from the pool.

Following is the sample health check configuration:

```
backend http_back balance roundrobin server web1
192.168.1.101:80 check fall 3 rise 2 server web2
192.168.1.102:80 check fall 3 rise 2
```

In the above code snippet,

- check: Enables health checks.
- fall 3: Server is considered down after 3 consecutive failed health checks.
- rise 2: Server is considered up after 2 consecutive successful health checks.

Monitoring and Managing Load Balancer

- Viewing HAProxy Logs:

Logs are configured in the **global** section of the HAProxy configuration. To view HAProxy logs:

```
$ tail -f /var/log/haproxy.log
```

- Enabling HAProxy Management Interface:

To enable the HAProxy management interface, add the following to the configuration:

```
frontend stats bind *:8404 stats enable stats uri / stats
refresh 10s stats auth admin:password
```

- Access the interface via `http://<your_server_ip>:8404`.

By using tools like HAProxy, sysadmins can easily configure and manage load balancers. Monitoring system load using tools like **top**, **htop**, **vmstat**, and **iostat** helps identify bottlenecks and optimize resource utilization. Advanced configurations such as least connections algorithm, SSL termination, and health checks provide robust and efficient load balancing solutions for large-scale deployments like AlphaProject.

Customizing Kernel

Kernel Customization Overview

Operating systems rely on their kernels to manage hardware resources and facilitate software-hardware communication. Improving security, adding new features, optimizing performance, and supporting specific hardware are all possible through kernel customization. This procedure incorporates user-defined modules, recompiles the kernel, and modifies kernel parameters.

Following are some situations where kernel customization may be necessary:

1. Performance Optimization: Tailoring the kernel to improve performance for specific workloads.
2. Hardware Support: Adding or enhancing support for new or specialized hardware.
3. Security Enhancements: Integrating security patches or hardening the kernel against vulnerabilities.
4. Feature Additions: Enabling or disabling specific kernel features based on project requirements.
5. Troubleshooting: Debugging and resolving issues related to kernel functionality.

Step-by-Step Customizing Kernel

Preparing the Environment

Ensure the system is updated and necessary packages are installed for kernel compilation.

```
$ sudo apt update $ sudo apt upgrade $ sudo apt install
build-essential libncurses-dev bison flex libssl-dev
libelf-dev
```

Downloading the Kernel Source

Download the latest or required kernel source from the official website.

```
$ wget
https://cdn.kernel.org/pub/linux/kernel/v5.x/linux-
5.10.1.tar.xz $ tar -xf linux-5.10.1.tar.xz $ cd linux-
5.10.1
```

Configuring the Kernel

Configure the kernel options. This can be done using a menu-driven interface.

```
$ make menuconfig
```

Navigating **`menuconfig`**:

- Processor Type and Features: Customize CPU-specific options.

- General Setup: General kernel settings.
- Device Drivers: Enable or disable support for specific hardware.
- File Systems: Include or exclude support for different file systems.
- Networking Support: Configure networking protocols and features.

Compiling the Kernel

Compile the kernel and its modules. This process can be time-consuming based on the system's capabilities.

```
$ make -j$(nproc) $ sudo make modules_install $ sudo make
install
```

Updating the Bootloader

Update the bootloader to include the new kernel. For systems using GRUB, update GRUB configuration.

```
$ sudo update-grub
```

Rebooting into the New Kernel

Reboot the system to use the newly compiled kernel.

```
$ sudo reboot
```

Verify the running kernel version after reboot.

```
$ uname -r
```

Sample Program: Kernel Customization for AlphaProject

Scenario 1: Enabling Specific Hardware Support

Imagine AlphaProject requires support for a specific piece of hardware not enabled by default. Following is how we enable it:

- Access **menuconfig**:

```
$ make menuconfig
```

- Navigate to Device Drivers: Find the specific driver for the hardware and enable it (denoted by **[*]**).
- Save Configuration: Save and exit **menuconfig**.
- Compile and Install the Kernel:

```
$ make -j$(nproc) $ sudo make modules_install $ sudo make install
```

- Update GRUB and Reboot:

```
$ sudo update-grub $ sudo reboot
```

Scenario 2: Applying Security Patches

For enhancing security, apply specific patches to the kernel.

- Download the Patch:

```
$ wget https://kernel.org/pub/linux/kernel/v5.x/patch-5.10.2.xz $ xz -d patch-5.10.2.xz $ patch -p1 < patch-5.10.2
```

- Reconfigure and Compile the Kernel:

```
$ make menuconfig $ make -j$(nproc) $ sudo make modules_install $ sudo make install
```

- Update GRUB and Reboot:

```
$ sudo update-grub $ sudo reboot
```

Scenario 3: Enabling Real-Time Kernel Features

For real-time applications, enable real-time features in the kernel.

- Access **menuconfig**:

```
$ make menuconfig
```

- Navigate to Processor Type and Features: Enable "Preemptible Kernel (Low-Latency Desktop)" or "Fully Preemptible Kernel (RT)".
- Save Configuration and Compile the Kernel:

```
$ make -j$(nproc) $ sudo make modules_install $ sudo make
install
```

- Update GRUB and Reboot:

```
$ sudo update-grub $ sudo reboot
```

Custom Kernel Modules

Writing a Simple Kernel Module

Kernel modules extend the functionality of the kernel without the need to reboot the system. Given below is how to write a simple "Hello World" kernel module.

- Create Module Source File:

```
// hello.c #include <linux/module.h> #include
<linux/kernel.h> #include <linux/init.h> static int
__init hello_init(void) { printk(KERN_INFO "Hello,
World!\n"); return 0; } static void __exit
hello_exit(void) { printk(KERN_INFO "Goodbye, World!\n");
} module_init(hello_init); module_exit(hello_exit);
MODULE_LICENSE("GPL"); MODULE_AUTHOR("Author Name");
MODULE_DESCRIPTION("A simple Hello World Kernel Module");
```

- Create Makefile:

```
# Makefile obj-m += hello.o all: make -C
/lib/modules/$(shell uname -r)/build M=$(PWD) modules
clean: make -C /lib/modules/$(shell uname -r)/build
M=$(PWD) clean
```

- Compile the Module:

```
$ make
```

- Insert the Module:

```
$ sudo insmod hello.ko $ dmesg | tail
```

You should see the message "Hello, World!" in the kernel log.

- Remove the Module:

```
$ sudo rmmod hello $ dmesg | tail
```

You should see the message "Goodbye, World!" in the kernel log.

By making changes to the kernel, system administrators can make the system work better for its users, make it work with new hardware, and make it more secure. It is important to prepare and test thoroughly before deploying these changes to make sure they are stable and compatible with current apps and workloads.

Summary

Managing large-scale deployments, dealing with Kubernetes, creating and maintaining clusters, implementing load balancing, and configuring the kernel were all topics covered in this chapter. First, the chapter provided a high-level outline of what is required for large-scale deployments, with an emphasis on scalability, automation, consistency, and availability. Using configuration management tools like Ansible and continuous integration and delivery platforms like Jenkins, practical techniques were shown for delivering AlphaProject at scale.

Following that, the groundbreaking container orchestration technology Kubernetes was unveiled, completely altering the way applications are deployed. We gained knowledge on how to set up a master node, connect worker nodes, and deploy a basic Nginx application to showcase Kubernetes' capabilities. We also learned how to install and configure Kubernetes on top of their current development environment.

To facilitate efficient communication and resource management among nodes, step-by-step instructions were provided for kubernetes configuration and setting up clusters for AlphaProject. We spoke about how to implement load balancing and why it is crucial to distribute traffic so that no one server becomes a bottleneck. Practical implementation was demonstrated using HAProxy, which included configuration, monitoring, and advanced scenarios such as SSL termination and health checks.

Kernel customization, which explains why you need to do it, was the last section of the chapter.

The steps to update the bootloader, configure and compile the kernel, and download the kernel source were detailed. Some real-world examples include enabling real-time capabilities, installing security patches, and enabling support for specific hardware. We also went over custom kernel modules, which allowed us to write, compile, and load a basic "Hello World" module with ease.

To sum up, this chapter provided you with the advanced knowledge and abilities needed to improve performance, boost security, and efficiently manage contemporary infrastructure in large-scale and complex environments using system administration.

Index

L

M

N

O

P

R

S

T

U

V

W

Y

Z

Epilogue

As we conclude this book, it's time to reflect on the extensive knowledge and skills you have gained throughout this journey. This book was designed to build on the foundational skills from *Linux Basics for SysAdmin* and elevate your expertise to handle the complex and demanding tasks of managing enterprise-level Linux environments.

The journey began with **Up and Running with System Administration Essentials**, a quick refresher to ensure you were prepared for the advanced topics. This chapter revisited key administrative tasks such as browsing files and directories, managing packages, using systemd, and configuring user profiles and permissions. This foundation ensured you were ready to dive deeper into more complex areas.

In **Managing Networks**, you explored the intricacies of network configuration and management. You learned to set up and manage network interfaces, configure IP addresses and routing, and handle essential services like DHCP and DNS. Using tools like Wireshark, you gained skills in network diagnostics and security, essential for maintaining robust network environments.

Security and Monitoring elevated your understanding of system security. You configured firewalls with **iptables** and **firewalld**, implemented AppArmor, and performed security audits with Lynis. You also set up intrusion detection systems like Snort and learned to monitor system logs for security issues. These skills are crucial for fortifying your systems against threats and ensuring compliance with security standards.

Database Management equipped you with the knowledge to handle databases in Linux environments, focusing on PostgreSQL. You mastered installation, configuration, database design, migrations, backup and restore procedures, and performance monitoring with Nagios. This chapter ensured you could manage and secure databases efficiently and effectively.

In **System Health Monitoring**, you delved into comprehensive monitoring techniques for various system resources. Using tools like **top**, **htop**, Nagios, and Zabbix, you learned to monitor CPU, memory, disk usage, and network performance. This chapter emphasized the importance of proactive monitoring and the ability to respond quickly to system performance issues, ensuring optimal system health and uptime.

Automation and Scripting enhanced your ability to automate routine tasks, manage resources, and perform system audits. You developed advanced scripting skills using shell scripting, **cron**, **anacron**, **awk**, and **sed**, significantly improving efficiency and consistency in system administration. This chapter highlighted the power of automation in reducing manual workloads and increasing system reliability.

Finally, **Advanced System Administration** explored managing large-scale deployments, Kubernetes, cluster management, load balancing, and kernel customization. These advanced topics prepared you to handle the most complex and demanding IT environments with confidence and expertise. You learned to deploy and manage applications at scale, ensure high availability, and optimize system performance through kernel customization.

Through these chapters, you have transformed into a highly capable and proficient system administrator. The skills and knowledge you have gained will enable you to confidently tackle any challenge in modern IT infrastructure. Whether managing a few servers or an extensive infrastructure, you now possess the expertise to ensure your systems are secure, efficient, and reliable.

This journey doesn't end here. The world of Linux is ever-evolving, and continuous learning is key to staying ahead. Keep exploring new technologies, tools, and techniques to further enhance your capabilities. This book serves as a cornerstone for your ongoing professional growth and expertise in Linux system administration. By mastering these advanced topics, you are well-equipped to manage and optimize large-scale Linux environments, ensuring their security, performance, and reliability.

Thank You

Printed in the USA
CPSIA information can be obtained
at www.ICGtesting.com
CBHW081708051224
18507CB00031B/870

9 788119 177851